CW00952364

PRAISE FOR "ENVISIONING HOLOGRAMS" BY AUTHOR, M. PELL

PELL IS A VISIONARY DESIGNER WHO HAS CREATED A MUST-READ FOR ANYONE MAKING CONTENT FOR THE HOLOLENS, MAGIC LEAP, OR ANY OTHER AR SYSTEM."

— Charlie Fink
Forbes Columnist, Consultant, Speaker, Author

ENVISIONING HOLOGRAMS IS A GUIDEBOOK FOR DESIGNING OUR HOLOGRAPHIC FUTURE THAT WILL CHANGE HOW WE WORK, PLAY AND COMMUNICATE."

— Tony Parisi
Global Head of AR/VR for Unity. Industry legend

DESIGN STUDENTS, THIS BOOK IS YOUR TREASURE MAP. DESIGN TEACHERS, MAKE THIS REQUIRED READING."

— Cynthia Andrews
Data Artist and Visualizer

THIS BOOK HELPS DEFINE A NEW DESIGN LANGUAGE FOR THIS WORLD-CHANGING MEDIUM."

— Ori Inbar
Managing Partner for Super Ventures, an AR/VR fund

ENVISIONING HOLOGRAMS IS AN EXCEPTIONAL INTRODUCTION TO A NEW WAY OF THINKING ABOUT SOFTWARE"

— Lucas Rizzotto
Award-winning creator of Mixed Reality experiences

I WAS TRULY ENTHRALLED READING ENVISIONING HOLOGRAMS. ITS CERTAINLY A FOUNDATIONAL BOOK FOR ME AND MY TEAM."

— Denise Elizabeth White
CEO of SPATIALx

The Age of
Smart Information

*How **Artificial Intelligence** and **Spatial Computing**
will transform the way we communicate forever*

M. Pell

Foreword by Charlie Fink

The Age of Smart Information

Designed, written, illustrated, and produced by **M. Pell**

ISBN-13: 978-1-7336870-4-1

First Edition, 2019
Printed in the USA

Published by

Futuristic Design, Inc.
Seattle | New York City

www.FuturisticDesign.com

This one is for you.

CONTENTS

BOOK SUMARY

The fundamental nature of Information
will be completely transformed by AI + XR

 **book**

by Charlie Fink

Our relationship to content, and the real world itself, is changing. As we enter this next phase of ubiquitous, invisible, and wearable computing, what was flat, now has dimensions. What was dead, is now alive, energized by AI and Spatial Computing. Mike Pell explains in the following pages how data, text, pictures, graphics, and anything else really, can be enabled to reveal deeper meaning, hidden relationships, and even tell its own story. In this book, Pell shares his compelling vision for the future of information and our most vital and humble communications tool – **text**.

Readers of Pell's first book, *Envisioning Holograms*, were given a unique look at the design thinking and approach taken when creating content for the then newly invented Microsoft HoloLens. As one of the creators of *Adobe Acrobat*, Pell has some experience with disruption, which makes him the right person to shed some light on what's coming next for us in the area of information design, consumption, and authoring.

Understanding the context of what's happening all around us now is key to comprehending the importance of this book. Most industry experts like myself subscribe to a few commonly held ideas. The first, and most important, is that Augmented Reality is the operating system for the real world. The world now has another layer or dimension, mediated by the camera, which is constantly digitizing and potentially altering all we see in real time. Writing in Wired, Kevin Kelly calls this the "Mirrorworld," the digital twin of our world, invisible to the naked eye. I call it a world painted with data. Magic Leap calls it "the Magicverse", and AWE founder and VC investor Ori Inbar calls it "Wikipedia for the real world," and so on. Lots of names, one idea. There's a vast invisible world that we are just now starting to surface.

Into this scenario comes Pell, fresh from his pioneering design work on Envisioning Holograms. His frequent lectures begin with the observation that we spend much of our time reading ordinary text on our computers and mobile devices, yet that textual aspect of communication hasn't changed at all in decades despite our daily technical advancements. He then asks his favorite question - how will text change in a more dimensional world? (like the ones we just talked about above). Would everything still really be a page?

Pell's belief is that the old way of reading 2D pages will be supplanted by a multi-dimensional experience. He predicts the page will soon become a "tired affordance" of the old world: lifeless, isolated, and dead as a tombstone. It's time for text to come alive and propel us toward what he calls *"The Age of Smart Information."*

This book predicts that in the near future, the data we regularly consume will feel like it's alive and aware, powered by a type of Artificial Intelligence that understands our routines, location, time of day, schedule, and even our emotions, to automatically filter how it is presented to us. New devices, together with precise geolocation and latency-free cloud computing, will be able to place information exactly where and when we need it, without us having to take any explicit action to make it happen. Pell believes this unique, personalized combination of Spatial Computing and Artificial Intelligence will enable our most common forms of communication to come to life right before our eyes.

"The beauty we seek is not found in first impressions, but rather in how the truth reveals itself," is Pell's poetic description of what the exploration of Smart Information allows. In this new world of Spatial Computing, containers of information will know how and when to reveal their hidden gems.

But, even when powered by a sophisticated AI, only humans can ascribe meaning and recognize value from any new delivery format. I experienced that effect myself during a mind-blowing demo at Augmented World Expo last year, where I found myself walking through Shakespeare's "*Hamlet*" using *Flow Immersive* in Virtual Reality. It was presented as a room-scale 3D forest of slowly animating words and the narrative's phrases, which gave me a new perspective on a classic work.

Through our frequent conversations over the last year, Pell has also opened my eyes to consider everyday actions I take for granted more closely, like talking, reading, and even my writing. Perhaps my words have deeper meaning of which I am not consciously aware. Or perhaps there's a better way for me to tell you all of this beside the written word. According to Pell, there is, and this inspiring book describes those possibilities.

Charlie Fink
Los Angeles, CA
November 2018

THE AGE OF

SMART

INFORMATION

Revolution Calling

Notes from your future

Looking back from January 2023, it's hard to imagine there was a time when the world's information was flat and lifeless, just sitting there, waiting to be understood.

Five event-filled years have passed since 2018, when Artificial Intelligence made its way into our everyday lives via useful Siri suggestions, Augmented Reality really hit the mainstream through our smartphone cameras, and people saw the true potential of Spatial Computing when cheap headsets became untethered.

Back then, an immeasurable number of text-based documents and images represented the sum total of civilization's knowledge and communication. Simply pixels on an electronic screen, all of our digital documents, books, mails, reports, data, songs, videos, and artwork just sat there, doing absolutely nothing. Why? At that point in time, our digital artifacts didn't know how to convey their own meaning, had no contextual awareness whatsoever, and were even missing the slightest bit of onboard intelligence. Remarkable given today's world of Smart Information, but back then it was nothing but unresponsive pixels.

Mountains of inert data and information kept growing, every day, everywhere. But more concerning than the raw pixel tonnage piling up was the fact that civilization's combined knowledge and wisdom was held captive within these inflexible digital prison cells. Even the best of our digital authoring tools kept creating relatively primitive representations of our important thoughts within "dumb" containers. Authoring anything more than a static container was too expensive timewise given the amount of effort required. Because content didn't ordinarily need to adapt itself to different forms to convey meaning, there was no automated way to create this capability back then.

The enlightened among us realized that for content's true value to be unleashed from within the containers of its original form, we needed a way to automate the immense amount of manual creation tasks required to create different representations. That laborious process alone kept this from happening for decades. Surprisingly, it seemed no one thought to question why we were fine with it for so long. But the truth is we didn't have all the right pieces in place yet. Until one day we finally realized what was possible by combining the emerging fields of AI and Spatial Computing – it was a bold experiment that could completely change the nature of communication forever.

By tackling the existing challenges with information and data containers, we could overcome its biggest limitations – (1) they were inert islands trapped within our most common digital artifacts, (2) they couldn't tell their own stories, (3) had no contextual or environmental awareness to adjust for relevance, and (4) required a dreadful manual creation process to produce custom forms for use in any channel other than the original.

With those challenges in mind, we set off to build the future. And just like that, almost overnight, we started to create a new type of "smart" information that could tell its own contextually-aware story, surface the invisible insights while conveying meaning, and make the non-obvious connections for people in ways that its digital predecessors or analog artifacts never could. Not a bad start, and spelled doom for all those dead pixels.

The Revolution

What began as a small set of experiments to leverage AI and Spatial Computing to power next-gen information experiences soon ignited the worldwide revolution in data design. It almost immediately shifted the way we were thinking about designing information and expanded our expectations of what was possible. We started using Machine Learning to identify data insights and Augmented Reality to surface meaning in new ways. It felt back then like a unique new communication language was born. The possibilities were limitless. We wasted no time.

Given the perspective of looking back at all this from 2023, the speed at which the transformation happened was startling. We saw our documents and photos come to life seemingly overnight, tweets instantly organized and amplified, and our most useful educational materials become more understandable at 10x the speed of other major technical revolutions. People felt smarter and more empowered without having to make any major changes to their daily habits or learn any new skills. The things we consumed every day became clearer, seemingly on their own. Responding to anything became a breeze thanks to the active assistance (first seen dramatically in Gmail finishing your sentences as you typed). It felt like mindreading had finally been perfected. Perhaps older generations would have found it unsettling and been concerned, but we embraced it because it came without effort and felt natural.

Once Designers learned of the amazing new palette they could create experiences with, there was no stopping them. Artists combined forces with Data Scientists, Developers with Marketers, and Cognitive Scientists with Evangelists to work on what felt like a new way of delivering impact and meaning. This explosion of creativity, engineering, and human ingenuity must have felt good at the time, but in a larger historical perspective it resembled a mini-Renaissance period.

And just like that, in the blink of an eye, we all were living in *The Age of Smart Information.*

From a historical technology perspective, Smart Information wasn't a brand new innovation with no prior art. It was the mashup of many existing technologies and approaches into a new object-oriented framework that did have some new-to-world capabilities. The presentation layer was put together with everything from simple HTML and web-based GUI libraries, to advanced XR rendering and display tech. The middleware was nothing out of the ordinary – the same services that ran large content-based operations. And the backend leveraged much of the work being done with AI in the form of Machine Learning analyzing patterns of consumption over time, and Reinforcement Learning constantly adjusting the experience to gain insight to predict future behavior. All that said, when combined together in clever new ways, these existing solutions did create a truly breakthrough experience.

The Impact

Even now, it's hard to quantify the overall impact that the Smart Information revolution had on society. Akin to the invention of moving pictures in the late 1800's, this technological and cultural transformation become so widespread and embedded in the fabric of life, that it would have been impossible to understand it's eventual magnitude while it was unfolding.

You can, however, easily observe the outcome – it literally changed everything about how we author and communicate. We moved quickly from a world of static artifacts and labor-intensive tasks to almost everything having the capability to tell its own story, autonomously, whether purely digital or attached to analog objects. And better yet, we didn't have to manually create all of it ourselves, every time.

When we learned how to leverage the power and speed of AI to assist us in creating multiple forms of the same message from one source, surface previously hidden insights, and do the heavy lifting of data analysis on our behalf, it was game on. Innovators went into overdrive. They quickly created and iteratively refined experiencing our information in multiple dimensions to better understand its intended meaning and take the appropriate action. The combination was stunning in its efficiency and beautiful to behold. Information was transformed from its historically lifeless forms into a new kind of living container.

Breakthroughs

Along the way to today's vibrant world of intelligent content, there were four major breakthroughs that jumpstarted and catalyzed the

Smart Information revolution. Each provided a key part of the puzzle and formed the platform's base.

Contextual awareness was a foundational element of those early experiences. It was obvious to the Smart Information pioneers that one of the most valuable things we could change about the existing content consumption experience was doing a better job of presenting things in the most appropriate form for the given situation. More than simply reflowing a web page for a particular device's screen size, this contextual awareness effort looked at where people were, what time of day it was, current activities, historical behavior, and the type of devices they had access to at the moment. Constructing a more complete picture of the current context, coupled with the ability to find or generate the most logically appropriate form of the message, spurred the development of a whole new delivery and consumption platform. It could enable information to feel more appropriate all the time.

Surfacing the invisible was the catchphrase used to describe showing previously hidden (or omitted) detail and insights in everything from throwaway tweets to our most heralded tomes. It also became a key pillar of the Smart Information movement. Showing what existed just below the surface or in the background was a true revelation to most people. We inherently know all of these things exist, but it was shocking to see how much people loved discovering these buried treasures when presented in this new way. No longer would the intended meaning of something remain obscure or exist only in the ether for the insightful – everyday people could now access all of it without much effort.

Most content started to be constructed in ways that made it easy to surface those invisible aspects in truly compelling ways without the reader or audience even needing to ask (if appropriate for the given circumstances). That's where the advanced AI came in – understanding what needed to be presented to give people the best chance of "getting it". That applied to everything from individual words all the way up to entire works.

The moment of clarity each of us experience when we encounter new ideas and concepts is a truly magical time. It's that exact second the proverbial light bulb goes on. We suddenly have a clear understanding of the idea or concept we've just been exposed to. Wow! Our brains seem to light up and our ego inflates just a bit as we're quite pleased to have made the connection. For millennia, creators of all sorts could never accurately predict when the moment of clarity would come for most people. If we cared to try, we guessed, and steered our work to lead to it. That's never an easy task – making the required connections, as all of us are so incredibly diverse in our thought processes, it's a small miracle we get people there at all.

To that end, one of the most important leaps forward in the pursuit of clarity was not only the ability to communicate at the right level of detail to be understood by a particular individual, but also learning over time what they responded to. By leveraging AI's Reinforcement Learning techniques to glean what particular aspects of information a person has responded well to in the past opened up a whole new approach to authoring for clarity and provided a playbook that worked. Once we became proficient at engineering the moment of clarity for people, amplified by our evolving toolsets, things just felt like they snapped into place. We got it. They got it. Everything was clicking.

Ambient intelligence came to be the industry term that we used to describe how our physical environments would light up to display the right info at the right time. Made it feel like the world around us was recognizing and understanding what we did and said. That was made possible thanks to AI being embedded into the very fabric of every device and surface we came into contact with in our travels. Although it's true that AI powered it all behind-the-scenes, the real star of that experience was the form of information that appeared – whether it was as a 3D holographic traffic indicator floating above your automobile's dashboard or a warning indicator projected onto a hot surface that appeared just as you reached anywhere near it. Our spaces were alive and paying attention to us in ways we never thought of.

Even from the earliest days of IoT and consumer-grade sensors like the Xbox Kinect, it sure felt like our future would involve interacting with "things" more often. The rise of Intelligent Assistants like Siri and Alexa cemented that into our daily routines. And now, our toasters ask us if we really meant to burn the bagel before continuing on. Our essays for class started writing themselves when we stalled out. The world seemed to know just what we needed and quietly started providing it without us needing to ask. Smart Information was the visual, auditory, and tactile layer underlying how we communicated.

The Experience

Given our penchant for machine-like efficiency and productivity when creating or consuming data, it's remarkable that *emotion* became the center of gravity for this new design direction. Moving past efficiency to impact, the way it felt when interacting with things dominated the industry conversation. It was a big change that warranted much discussion and analysis within multiple industries.

The following aspects of the overall Smart Information experience came out of those discussions and experiments with emotion, which helped us move beyond the rudimentary layout and interaction models of the past onto dynamic, living pieces that made a real connection with people.

Design thinking was critical in making this leap forward. Design has always been just as transformational as technology in these types of leaps, but it's harder to spot in action. We know when something is suddenly possible (technology), yet the way it behaves, looks, feels, and acts (design) is somehow less interesting or apparent to the average person (unless it reduces friction or pain). That situation reversed itself quickly during the early days of Smart Information. Great visual and interaction design were clearly evident and noticed right away. The way these digital artifacts appeared and felt when we interacted with them was unmistakably new. It felt good. The technology was unimportant compared to the engaging design.

Suddenly, our words, images, sounds, and physical attributes went from unremarkable in their normal resting state within information instances, to embodying unmistakable energy and demanding attention. The design also leveraged a whole new gestural language and interaction model for active communication and deep exploration. Previously activated only by our intellect and imagination, highly designed narratives and revelations began to flow from our most common digital artifacts. The future of information became a hotspot of activity and reward for creators and consumers.

Behavior is recognized as being primarily responsible for whether we deeply love or absolutely can't stand something from an experience standpoint. Visuals and first impressions will always play a huge role in satisfaction, but an object's behavior determines our willingness to further engage or immediately bail. It is the small things in how something acts that sets them apart.

From a behavioral design standpoint, the hallmark of the Smart Information experience was its uncanny ability to communicate effortlessly at the right altitude or level of detail for a given situation. For any given audience, that behavior is what endeared them to the medium. Hands down. Whatever was being created or consumed felt dialed in for that exact moment and situation. Add to that the ability to dynamically adapt to changing conditions and circumstances, and you have a predictable pattern of behavior that's pleasing to your audience. People ate it up. There was no going back.

Intelligence was never thought of as a property of information itself before this revolution. In fact, that would have seemed quite odd given our focus historically on integrating intelligence into our systems, not their output. Yet, much of what we consider to be normal or expected intelligence now resides within the artifact or object itself, not the system delivering it (even though it does exist within both many times). That shift was not possible before our services, systems, and toolsets were updated to use Artificial Intelligence and Machine Learning models to extract and amplify the underlying structure and value of the content or data. "Intelligence On Board" was the bumper sticker du jour.

The tasks required to identify insights and create clarity ran like invisible engines in the background of any active encounter with information. Further enhancing that feeling of intelligence on board was the use of AI's Reinforcement Learning techniques to track what we responded to during sessions. These incredible feats of "intelligence" were regularly accomplished by processing real-time input streams. It felt nothing short of miraculous compared to the manual number crunching and analysis tasks of the first Productivity Age.

Ethics is perhaps the most overlooked and misunderstood part of the Smart Information universe. One of the biggest issues that came along with Artificial Intelligence being embedded within our common information was the notion that our systems needed to have integrity, a conscience, and moral compass. We are a fair and just society in principle, so why wouldn't we strive to model our AI systems in that image? We did try our best to be ethical in code, yet unconscious bias permeated the systems and algorithms we created since the dawn of the computer. We taught our models poorly at first, but eventually recognized how to identify and remove bias to form a more transparent and solid ethical base to operate from. We eventually let the content make decisions on a local basis, informed by a centralized moral compass. Worked out well for most cases, but it remains an ongoing issue.

This same "local decisions informed by a central policy" approach was also used for privacy, security, and safety issues being handled by the Smart Information delivery and consumption systems. The resulting distributed code of conduct faced some difficult challenges when trying to determine how information should conduct itself. It also needed to deal with how to treat people properly given the current context and environment. No easy answers there, but we are evolving our systems to be more empathetic and less rules based.

The System

No technological change of this magnitude could happen without some of the appropriate infrastructure already existing or being built as needed. Just as with Web technologies like the HTTP protocol, HTML markup language, and JavaScript programming language powering the rise of the World Wide Web, so too did Smart Information have its foundational elements.

From a system perspective, **Artificial Intelligence** and **Mixed Reality** were the two key system elements that fueled the initial growth of Smart Information implementations. Both fields of study and implementations were on fire before any of this took off, and once combined, they turned this movement into something completely different. This was the hottest place to work for awhile. Many critical system parts still needed to be envisioned, forged, and deployed one-by-one – but the evidence of major impact those had was easily apparent from the earliest experiments. Information systems were cast in a completely new light (more complementary I must say). The result was breathtaking and humbling. A new kind of reality become visible to all of us, almost at once.

In the beginning, small teams of brilliant individuals and straight up hackers created the first (relatively) crude tools and platforms to test out system-level hacks. Far from revolution igniting work, these were just clever experiments to test proof of concept pieces. That said, they immediately showed the potential leap forward we were all about to make. And little did we know it would go worldwide almost in an instant, and end up being completely transformative.

Constructs are the invisible building blocks of our digital systems that hold everything together behind-the-scenes. To system architects and programmers, these constructs are elegant packaging for organized thought. You can see their eyes light up when describing them in hushed tones and reverence. Representing structured thoughts that have become codified, constructs hold the individual parts of our Smart Information objects together and allow them to operate with real efficiency.

For the rest of us, constructs are invisible, and assuredly boring detail of a technology solution that seems mind-bogglingly complex. That said, we all owe many of the giant leaps forward we've made in communicating to the forethought and beauty put into those clever constructs. They are in many respects the key reason we were able to advance past the lifeless containers and frameworks of the past. Structure matters.

Technologies that enabled the rise of Smart Information were developed for very different purposes before combining to power this revolution.

The foundational element of most business and educational communication is some form of written language. The words themselves were merely ASCII characters stored in an electronic file prior to the advent of Smart Information. The key constructs developed during this period such as *Information Objects* quickly evolved into the multi-dimensional, connected, intelligent containers that power most of the world's communication today in 2023. Interoperable, componentized, and modular, words are now far more than simple marks on a page thanks to the constructs that were devised to enable stunning representations of their meaning, connections, relationships, and levels of detail.

Artificial Intelligence gave us the ability to process data, look for patterns and trends, and monitor systems on our behalf. The aspect of AI that really fueled the growth of Smart Information was the ability to better understand how people wanted to be communicated to for a given situation. That contextual relevance was missing in most common forms of interaction. We were very one dimensional in our approach prior to this, no pun intended.

Augmented Reality and its related Spatial technologies provided us a way to see the invisible elements of our information and add additional data to objects in the real world. Although AR was not required for many levels of detail to function, the ability to use audio, video, tactile, and dimensional technologies to communicate things in multiple ways at once ignited a goldrush to find and monetize efficient ways to combine these disparate solutions into compact and efficient delivery vehicles.

Cloud Computing became indispensable initially by running the services that allowed us to store and share our things with each other, regardless of what type of device were using from anywhere in the world. Over time, it became apparent that we needed to add spatial permanence and landmarks to our information, so we could understand better where things came from and belonged. That prompted the advent of the *AR Cloud* to not only store locational aspects, but also do the computation and processing of multi-level representations of our information. We could not have the interconnectedness, relationships, and interoperability of Smart Information without Cloud Computing.

Platforms always serve as the underpinnings of our systems and services. They make rapid scalability and extreme growth possible by providing a stable foundation for developers and architects to build upon. In the case of Smart Information, the key platform work that was done enabled both a consistent frontend experience (Cloud-based presentation and interaction processing) and powerful backend processing (Cloud-based AI and ML) to leverage tons of existing work.

All the same behaviors and computing could be done locally, but using a ubiquitous online platform opened up the possibilities for everyone, not just those who installed a particular set of software. Platform as a Service (PaaS) was key in the rapid adoption of Smart Information solutions by content providers and publishers.

Tools were also very integral to the growth and adoption of this movement. Our traditional toolsets rapidly adopted the key technologies needed for Smart Information and built upon the platforms we developed along the way to provide a seamless experience for both authors and consumers. It was way smoother in many regards than any previous disruptive change to the computing landscape (perhaps we were getting pretty good at disruption by then). We seemed to have learned our lesson about creating brand new approaches vs. leveraging existing, well-understood methods. Smart Information rode in on the latter. We got the tooling part of the equation right because we built in the ability for information to appear in multiple forms within the playback platform, not requiring anything new or different.

The most significant shift in our use of tooling for Smart Information was the move away from thinking we needed to manually create every representation ourselves – the machine could now be trusted to do a good job of most operations. For decades, we always assumed if something needed to exist, we'd end up creating it ourselves. No more. Our tools could now take care of generating multiple high-quality representations of the same object automatically. It was done surprisingly well, in fact. Audio was generated by text-to-speech synthesizers using human voice (your own if you cared to train the tooling just a bit by reading a paragraph out loud and creating a "voice font"). Various visual representations were auto-generated using AI-powered design agents. Interaction models were standardized at the platform level and added automatically by the toolsets you were using to create the original version of something. Content even appeared in fully translated forms depending on the location it was consumed in. Imagine any tweet you wrote being available in dozens of languages without you knowing how to speak or read any of them. Tools were no longer thought of as something experts had to fly, but rather an approachable interaction with a trusted friend, albeit a know-it-all.

The Future

From Silicon Valley to New York City, Moscow to Hyderabad, London to Beijing, eventually every corner of the world will experience that deep emotional connection to their content that the Smart Information revolution enabled. Even traditionally dry topics will come to life in amazing new ways. The familiar will be experienced in the most appropriate way to make that connection with the person viewing or creating it. One by one, every new piece of information will become available in these new ways – and we will generally think nothing of it. In the future, as always, our children will assume it had always existed this way, because honestly, why wouldn't it?

The Smart Information revolution will continue on in new and completely unexpected ways, which will unquestionably lead to some major societal transitions for all of us and our descendants.

Smart Data will be the next logical extension of Smart Information. Recognizing the vast potential for adding value to data itself, we will drive more context and relational information into the exabytes of discreet datapoints we collect every second of every day. This will in turn cause an exponential increase in the amount of storage, compute power, and bandwidth required to keep pace with our expanding appetite. Just when we thought the Cloud would save us, it will become clear we bet our future on something we can easily cripple through our own complacency and ambition.

Smarter People are a natural outcome of the world's information being available in any form we desire to experience it in. Conversations get more insightful, and less superficial. Understanding goes deeper. Communication improves across the board, regardless of personality or ability to be articulate. As a species, we will further develop the ability to parallel process multiple streams of input and understand them concurrently (as we do already with more visceral input). This ability was something the teenagers of the world seemed to master a decade earlier, but it wasn't true. They were multi-tasking, not processing multiple sources with equal quality across them – that part is new. As always, we'll find ways to undermine our new abilities as our animal instincts stay intact, unfazed by the ability to generate and understand higher level discourse. We are humans after all.

Smartest World is the term used to talk about the explosion of ambient computing and environmental awareness woven into the spaces we inhabit. It won't be long before children are born who didn't realize there was a time when you couldn't talk with anything and everything, and expect an appropriate response. Life is recorded, rewindable, and able to be summoned at will. Smart Information fuels the way we experience that world, so we need to be careful to avoid all of the dystopian info overload clichés we envisioned when we first realized the experiential vector we were headed down. Human ingenuity, morals, and love will triumph over the soulless optimization of our technology-powered assistants / guardians, creating the best world we can hope for given our human nature.

The Journey

With all of that as the setup, this book takes you on a quick trip through all the topics we just touched that contributed to igniting the Smart Information revolution. You'll see how this foundational transformation resulted in a giant leap forward in our ability to communicate and be understood.

My hope is that by talking through all this with you, we can clearly see where this work will ultimately lead us to, together.

M. Pell
Seattle, WA
January 2023

PART 1

THE
IMPACT

THE AGE OF SMART INFORMATION

It's Alive

Our relationship with text has changed forever

There was a time when words were simply markings on a printed page or dead pixels on a screen.

Lifeless, flat, and disconnected, text passages required us to make sense of them and their intended meaning every single time we encountered them. They were simultaneously the best example of a human communication tool and yet the most demanding of any of our mediums. The clarity and beauty of those characters were realized only after our minds transformed those simple marks into an invisible film of our own design, unique to ourselves.

Until now.

The quite ordinary and generally unremarkable text we have always used to write down our best stories, worst news, snarky tweets, and everything else in between, is now capable of coming to life like some newly activated sci-fi *Transformer*, bursting off the page and into our world in any form that makes most sense given our current situation. It speaks up only when it needs to, making sure you know exactly what its intention and point is. We like to ask it questions, and it responds just like a person would.

[Enter]

This is the kind of change best experienced instead of talked about.

 Text is finally much more than just marks on a page. As an example, let's take a page from this book to illustrate what entering *The Age of Smart Information* feels like in comparison to our traditional book formats.

Just point your smartphone camera at the mark above and you'll have an opportunity to see part of this book immersively in a 3D browser or Virtual Reality if you have a headset handy.

Who knew ordinary book text could be injected with such life and behaviors? We have all seen glimpses of similar things in high tech company "vision videos" over the years, and certainly in sci-fi movie special effects reels, but it wasn't until the availability of Augmented Reality on our smartphones that people could see things come to life for themselves.

Whether through playful selfie camera filters, pointing the phone at a magazine cover to glimpse a *Harry Potter* type live photo, or watching some 3D animated characters telling us interesting anecdotes, people eventually started realizing the boring objects we took for granted could suddenly be energized by Spatial Computing technologies.

Books can include immersive experiences to augment the text

What started as a simple augmentation of words and passages using 3D models you could spin and examine, quickly evolved into different types of digital advertising using AR and VR. Those 3D ads felt more like mini-experiences that were very successful at demonstrating what those technologies are really great at – immersion. The only problem was that the vast majority of our communication (in the form of text) still sat there, doing nothing.

[Backspace]

Let's back up a just bit. Our written language has always been just a collection of words and phrases that we mentally piece together to create meaning. Yes, it could be beautiful at times, but that came from the way we interpreted it. Our minds created the imagery, divined its meaning, and assigned relative importance to those little glyphs. But at the same time, we missed some things, skipped over a ton of it, and really didn't understand our fair share. That said, it never really mattered because text on the page wasn't a living thing we had to actively deal with.

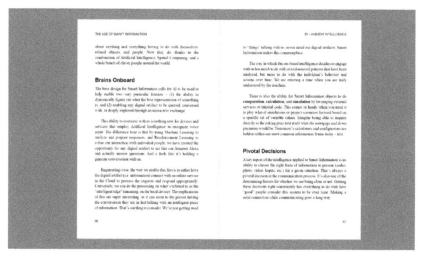

Our books have remained the same almost from inception

There was no two-way exchange or direct feedback to judge whether or not we "got it". Text just sat there. We were in control of whether to pay attention or disregard it. Then things changed in the most profound way… Smart Information started to appear and spread out across our common interactions.

This transformation didn't happen overnight, but it kinda felt like it did. One day we were all chill watching *Netflix* and catching up on our social feeds, and the next thing you know everyone is hysterically screaming about how AI is invading our lives and threatening to take over humanity (it did actually, in the form of *Alexa*, *Siri*, and public surveillance, but that's beside the point). And then the kids started playing that freaky *Beat Saber* VR game that looks like they're actually inside *Tron* stylishly dance battling with dual lightsabers. #unreal. Hard to believe, but those two seemingly unrelated trends combined to bring our text to life. Unlikely, but it's exactly how it happened.

When we realized how powerful and widespread Artificial Intelligence had become in such a short period of time, and how emotionally involved we were when engaged with virtual reality, it clicked. What if we combined these two forces together and applied them to the most important aspect of our lives? What would happen? Would the written language we use all day long to communicate be better with VR and AI?

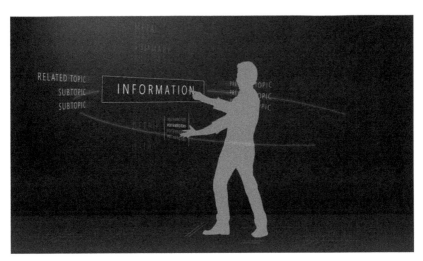

The fundamentals of information shifted due to AI + XR

What followed immediately after that realization is what this entire book is about – the thinking, methods, and tech used to shift from information's static past to its dynamic future. We're now racing at breakneck speeds to uncover ways to bring our ideas expressed in text to life by combining the power of AI with the emotional engagement of Spatial Computing or XR ("X" being all the things that come before "Reality" – Augmented, Mixed,

Virtual). This isn't merely creating 3D objects that dance on top of our static words, though.

The things we activate in this way will be powered by the same kind of intelligence as our digital assistants, and will be just as aware of our surroundings as a car's external sensors are for reading the real world. This continuous augmentation will be blended into our environments as much or little as is called for.

Familiar information is augmented seamlessly

Words can still be ignored, of course, but why would you when they speak to us in exactly the right way given what the current situation calls for. In the Age of Smart Information, text is tuned into our needs, and knows how we best deal with input at certain times of day and in particular places. It recognizes our language and mood and acts accordingly. And what really blows your mind is how it uncannily knows when to morph itself into a picture, animated diagram, video clip, or holographic experience to best communicate its message or convey a particular meaning. Text is no longer just a bunch of characters. It's alive.

And while we're at it, we'll expand this journey beyond words to include anything we communicate with, such as pictures, video, animations, spoken language, music, art, and even data. Anything can be enhanced in this way. The possibilities are limitless.

[Insert]

Let's insert a bit more formal definition at this point. The general term I use to describe **the experiential evolution of text** (and by extension, our other most common types of communication) is *Smart Information*. It's meant to capture the notion that things are no longer passive blobs of ink and pixels. They are alive, paying attention, and ready to interact with us. For me, information is defined broadly to include anything from a single data point, to individual words, tweets, documents, diagrams, reports, songs, videos, and up to entire collections of things. Information has never been just facts and figures, charts and diagrams, data and numbers. It's also the sum total of what you gain from engaging with it.

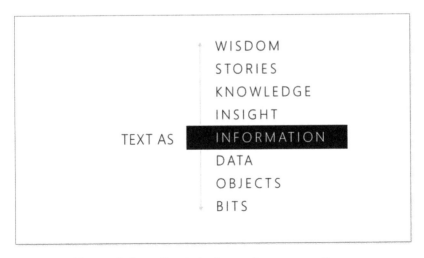

Text as Information is just one step on a continuum

That's where Smart Information differs and excels – it injects much more into the consumption stage than you'd normally expect to find from the same object in an older time. These newly supercharged experiences enable us to divine meaning and form understandable mental models for things that we may have overlooked or misunderstood in the past.

[Shift   ]

There are **five experiential attributes** that best illustrate the shift from the old world of completely dead content (that we needed to make sense of ourselves each time we encounter it), to the new world of Smart Information (that can tell its own story in multiple ways).

Experiential Attributes

- ▶ Contextual Awareness
- ▶ Dynamic Behavior
- ▶ Emotional Engagement
- ▶ Perceived Relationship
- ▶ Stunning Presentation

Contextual Awareness

Be aware of your surroundings. Isn't that what your mom always used to tell you before you headed into the big city? The most important aspect of Smart Information is that it's paying attention. It creates the feeling of being tuned in your exact circumstances (aka "context"). That doesn't come easy. There's an awful lot of complexity to the Artificial Intelligence and sensor tech behind being contextually-aware. It essentially allows it to figure out in real-time what form the message needs to take, and at what altitude it should be delivered at.

In everyday life, when we're spoken to at the wrong level of detail (i.e. too technical, overly simplistic, etc.) we tend to tune out immediately. Similarly, when we don't connect with the person listening due to presentation method (i.e. lecture, super dense writing, jargon slides, boring videos) we also stop paying attention quickly. The advancement Smart Information brings to this situation is ensuring delivery of the message in a way that makes sense and is welcome at this particular moment, for this specific place.

Your current context combines many different factors

That contextual awareness is accomplished by analyzing the environment and current situation before auto-selecting the right level of detail and presentation path. That sounds like magic perhaps, but it's what has been happening in our smartphones and cars for years. It has gotten so deeply integrated and natural we barely notice any longer. You didn't ask your smartphone how long it was going to take to get home, but you appreciate when it told you after heading there right? That's a great example of a Smart Information experience. Timely, useful, clever.

In the background, sensors and AI work together to determine the optimal style of communication and delivery method to use based on your current context. Coupled with a flexible presentation system that enables you to get the transmission verbally, visually, spatially (or in the most appropriate other form), the system delivers something that feels right for the given conditions. That level of understanding and environmental context is a giant leap forward for our formerly lifeless text. You could say this achievement of our content becoming self-aware was indeed its "Skynet moment".

Dynamic Behavior

Remember being surprised when *Siri* asked you a question with a slightly snarky tone? Unexpected, but fun. It's as if she knew you'd be ok with that response given your close relationship. At that moment, she didn't feel like a computer program just reading from a database of answers – she was more like a person being a bit lighthearted. That's the feeling we're after experientially, and why dynamic behavior is so important to Smart Information.

Information monitors its surroundings, just like a robot's sensors

Having an encounter with something that provides truly dynamic responses and produces welcome outcomes (based on your current situation) is exactly what digital assistant designers, researchers, and engineers have been working toward for decades. Note that a "dynamic" response doesn't mean its behavior isn't predictable once you become familiar with it. After all, we do rely on our world being predictable for the most part. Smart Information knows that, and optimizes for it.

It's still quite unusual for an ordinary document or other piece of information to suddenly spring to life or be able to interact with us as if it were a sentient object – it's unexpected and perhaps even unwanted. So, we need to be careful when applying this dynamic behavior. It should kick in only when you engage the information in a way that deserves an interaction and response like that. Many things should still sit there just as they always have, waiting to be understood. But, if it becomes clear there's something of value they can provide for us, they should spring into action pro-actively. As we'll soon discuss, these objects learn over time what we value and don't in this type of engagement.

Emotional Engagement

An elusive goal of experience designers everywhere is to create authentic emotional connections with objects, devices, and processes. Producing a feeling of love for something that's not a person is much harder to achieve than it sounds, trust me. Especially when we're all a bit jaded when it comes to being impressed by a given piece of tech these days. There's a new miracle in the modern world just about every news cycle. We have almost lost our ability to be surprised and amazed because of the sheer quantity of innovations making it to us on a regular basis. And that dulling of our amazement makes it even more difficult to create a strong emotional bond.

Our relationship with information and assistants is getting emotional

That said, there are some things (like Smart Information and Holograms) that have a built-in advantage – they elicit emotions just by us being exposed to them. Hard to scientifically explain, but clear as day to observe. We are naturally drawn to them due in part to the wonder and magic of the unexpected, and genuine thrill of learning something new in a deeply experiential way. Almost no one expects an ordinary piece of text in a tweet to be the onramp to an immersive, engaging, and perhaps heartwarming rabbit hole experience. Yet, it happens with Smart Information.

Just as with any type of Spatial Computing, magic and surprise are used to forge emotional bonds quickly in this design space. They're used like power ups in a game level, employing every trick you can think of to endear content to its intended audience. And that starts with a shift in perception.

Perceived Relationship

It's possible that the biggest change of this content revolution is not awareness, behavior, or emotion – but rather the monumental shift in our perception of what's now possible and the *relationship* that forms as a result. All living creatures are capable of bonding with things that interest, annoy, or excite them. This major behavioral change in our most common pieces of information has moved us closer to enjoying the type of relationship we have with our digital assistants and trusted devices. They "exist" in some other way that they didn't before.

People often say they love a particular book or movie because they felt something when first experiencing it, and it moved them. They might dress up cosplay style to show others their devotion, but for the most part, a film wasn't something they had an actual back-and-forth relationship with. Unrequited love perhaps. But, that all changes with Smart Information (although it may be on a much smaller scale). Documents can read themselves to us and answer our questions directly. Tweets help us understand the context of the expression and how others are reacting to it. Photos transport us to where they were taken for a sense of place. Books help us get through them rather than re-reading the same chapter over and over. And most importantly, a new understanding forms about our relationship to content and its role in our lives.

In the not too distant future, our most frequent interactions and conversations may well be with our devices and information rather than with real people. Oh wait, that already happened…

Stunning Presentation

Never before in human history have we been able to present our ideas, concepts, stories, diagrams, or heartfelt emotions with such impact. We have so many new ways to depict them it's difficult to choose which would be most clear and memorable. Starting with something as simple as text and instantly transforming it into a fully immersive adventure within Virtual Reality was only found in Sci-Fi movies not too long ago. Today, it's all around us. VR headsets are finally commodity priced and readily available, and everyone is already walking around with Augmented Reality enabled smartphones. We listen to audio books on our commutes, talk to holographic agents in airports, watch movies on tablets, and even silently respond to our watches when they ask for attention.

Smart Information as an immersive experience

We are awash in stunning presentation technologies and devices, all of which should be considered no less than magic compared to what existed a few short years ago. As storytellers, educators, and artists, our palettes are overflowing with vibrant paint and our minds bursting with creativity when thinking about how to best communicate in this Age of Smart Information.

[End]

In the end, we took text from being lifeless and passive, to feeling vibrant and alive. What was never really considered more than a bunch of words is now a trusted advisor. And what we tended to always take for granted is now a big part of the conversation. Text is no longer just a means of marking our thoughts onto pages and screens. Our words have come to life, helping reveal the thoughts, feelings, and wonder of their authors.

Surfacing
the Invisible

"There's more to the picture than meets the eye."
– Neil Young

Everything has a hidden story.

So many fascinating things in life are found just below the surface. Others are hiding in plain sight. Whether we're talking about a familiar person, photo, song, or even a leaf, there are so many aspects of the objects in our world that we never notice in the daily hustle of our lives. Everything has its own set of obscured facts, relationships, historical data, and connections that aren't easy to explore today, even if we wanted to. We're just not setup to handle that kind of decloaking in a quick way. But not for long…

I'll use a tired (but effective) iceberg metaphor here to make a point. The proverbial tip of the iceberg is the only visible part of a gigantic entity lurking just below the surface. You instinctively know there's more to it. And you know you could see it if you used some type of sonar or imaging equipment. Regardless, it's there. And that's exactly how you can think about a piece of Smart Information. There's a visible or auditory representation available now, but you know there's even more to it we're not seeing just yet. Now you're starting to get the idea of Smart Information's ability to handily encapsulate a tremendous amount of data about each thing it represents. There literally is more to it below the surface.

Levels of Detail

Having access to tons of data about something is one thing, but being able to clearly communicate an intended message about it effectively is another thing altogether. That requires making the right connection with the person on the receiving end. Always easier said than done, clear communication takes an understanding of audience to choose the right form and level of detail. Combine that with our desired goal of always being contextually relevant, and that's a tall order for any author of any piece of information.

One mistake we often make when creating a message is trying to pick and use the "one size fits all" form for everyone (and every situation), instead of creating multiple representations for each type of common scenario. It's natural to skip past generating multiple forms because it's a highly manual process today, and there's no easy way of picking which one to use for a particular scenario *at the time it is consumed.* That said, if you could observe people's consumption behavior, you would see a pattern emerge for the amount of detail they like given certain situations and types of information. That's what we're interested in being able to produce on-demand to align with most desirable forms.

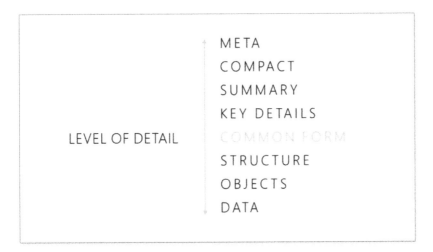

Levels of Detail range from highest level to most detail

In order to achieve that goal of a personalized, contextually aware, and targeted message, we'll first need to make available several different "levels of detail" to help the audience understand the material from different altitudes. These levels of detail go from minimal high-level summaries and overviews to super esoteric data. Conceptually, individual layers of information stack (like plates) so they can be switched into and out of at any time, for any part of the information being consumed.

Each layer serves as the right representation at a particular time for a piece of information based on the current context and the person viewing the material. There can be as many or as few levels of detail associated with an entity as needed for the job. It's not required to have all of them (or even more than one), but the more that exist the easier it will be to make that connection with people at the right level for them.

Level of Detail

These are various altitudes that we can view information at.

▸ Meta
▸ Compact
▸ Summary
▸ Key Details
▸ Common Form
▸ Structure
▸ Objects
▸ Data

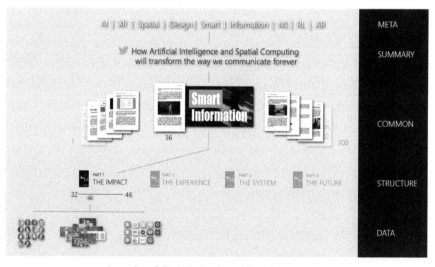

Levels of Detail depicted for this book

Meta level

More of a functional level than a useful consumption mode, the Meta level contains what you'd normally think of as keywords or search terms that help locate this artifact on the Web. It can be used to get a good idea of the general words that describe the objects.

Compact level

If you had to boil down an entire digital artifact into just one sentence, this would be the form that represents it. Being concise, brief, yet descriptive is the challenge for this particular level. Used mainly by other systems to list objects in catalogs or collections, this level is great for quick overviews and scans.

Summary level

Some people naturally prefer the summary or overview level of detail as a default view regardless to make things quick and easy. Starting at that overview level gives you a good feel for the key points of the message. That could come in the form of metadata keywords, or just a few sentences and short phrases to promote scanability. This level gives people the chance to glean the important aspects without much investment.

Presentation level

Moving down the stack one level, the different presentation layers provides a narrative. Supported by diagrams and animations as needed, this form would be most effective in getting the message across in an entertaining and engaging way for both serious pieces and fiction. This level uses different types of storytelling to deliver the content's essence while staying true to the nature or genre. For example, you could imagine an Augmented Reality vignette overlaying some element of the information to make the content more accessible or enjoyable.

Original form

The original form of the piece is always special. Even though we say anything is available, as any layer, at any time, the form it natively comes in is highly important. It gives people access to the author's intended layout, flow, and impression. There's a real possibility that people will gravitate toward a particular level of detail and perhaps never see the original form, but it's incredibly important to always have that original available to understand the base form. In the not too distant future, our artifacts will be natively multi-dimensional entities, making the original form doubly interesting to audiences who regularly get their own preferred level of detail rather than the original.

Detail level

And finally, a deeper level of detail is available on-demand to provide easy access to underlying data sets, related content, and in-depth treatments. This level is often jumped into for specific tasks related to data analysis, checking the content's source, or getting a deeper understanding of the material presented. Imagine an exploded 3D view of a complex mechanism, like an engine, and you get the idea of how powerful this level can be. Not generally thought of as the default view, but it could be.

All of these different levels of detail have their strengths and challenges. That's why we don't always suggest one by default, but try to glean the correct one for the particular person consuming the information. One size never fits all for Smart Information.

Hidden Data

We know there's always something "behind" a statement or piece of information. Sometimes it's a set of facts or data, other times it is opinion synthesized by experience. Regardless, people are often curious about the original source, underlying data, or responsible catalyst. It's partially why we ask so many questions and remain skeptical of assertions with no backing data. It's also why so regularly footnotes and citations are found supporting statements and figures to allow validation or deeper inspection. We are surfacing a hidden source to lend credibility to a statement.

Common Form   Structure   Data

This artwork by Sharon Pell-Lie hides multiple layers of information

Artwork is another great example of how applying the thinking behind Smart Information could reveal more in each piece. In Sharon Pell-Lie's mixed media artwork, each successive layer has a very particular purpose – a map serves as the base or Data layer, charcoal lines define the Structure layer, and finally the acrylic paint applied to both underlying layers produces the Common Form. It's all there, just obscured within the finished piece.

In a very different example, it's a common practice in business to make the spreadsheet data available for a series of charts or graphs if we believe it would benefit the person consuming it. We'd normally not lead with the underlying data in a presentation, but it's there if and when we need it. The inverse is also true – when you're in a meeting and someone asserts some dubious numbers as "data", you could easily challenge them to produce the actual underlying numbers for their claims because they'd be built into the model. Yeah, nice try buddy ;-)

In the same way, given our common desire to know more about *everything*, it's only natural to want to associate the additional data and related elements with each piece of Smart Information to provide the ability to explore where something came from or what's behind it. These supporting pieces of data are hidden by default but can always be shown when appropriate or asked for on-demand.

From an experiential perspective, access to hidden data is quick, fluid, and feels like a natural extension to the existing form. Available programmatically, these additional sub data elements are also consumed by automated systems rather than real people.

It is unclear where many elements of our most commonly used communications come from since they do not explicitly spell it out, but that doesn't prevent us from forming our own ideas based on education and life experiences. The change here with Smart Information is having a built-in ability to see where those elements came from through hidden metadata that identifies the source. Overkill for many things, but critical for others given our current problem of counterfeit media and stories.

Visualizing Flow

Some of us are visual thinkers who tend to mentally generate imagery for abstract concepts and ideas as part of our understanding process. That ability isn't one that everyone has in the same way, so another valuable capability of Smart Information is modeled on providing a visual representation of invisible ideas.

For example, being able to visualize the movement and motion of unseen forces and effects over time greatly aids in understanding them. Seeing a visual representation of something not usually that apparent gets the light bulb to appear more often than not.

Invisible sensor scans help this robot navigate

You have probably seen images of imperceptible waves or patterns being overlaid onto quite familiar settings, like Wi-Fi network signals permeating a room. It looks like a topographic map of a mountainous region. Even though these waves are invisible to the naked eye, they make perfect sense when we can illustrate and simulate how they move for people. Most of us wouldn't necessarily know what they looked like or in some cases that they were even present at all. That ability to visualize and conceptualize something that exists but is never seen by the naked eye is game changing. It always feels magical.

A considerable amount of effort is being applied to how we can auto-generate the world of unseen forces and movement with animated simulations in hopes of increasing our understanding of them. This has traditionally been a super time-consuming and compute intensive task to simulate physics and the real world, but there are many great tools and examples of doing this emerging.

An example of this type of visualization is when you see the projected weather patterns for the coming day or so. Those invisible forces like wind and offshore flow become relatively easy to understand colorful animations behind the weather person to enhance the predication that it will be windy tomorrow. We can always just rely on the simple word "Windy", but seeing the numbers and flow illustrated makes in more visceral and urgent.

Whenever we get a chance to see the invisible forces in our world surfaced in understandable ways, we have transcended our basic physical capability and should consider it a real win for human ingenuity.

The Moment of Clarity

It's about time we engineered getting to "a-ha"

The exact moment when something suddenly comes into focus and we truly "get it" is priceless. We love that feeling. Everything makes perfect sense. It's exhilarating when it happens and is usually accompanied by a temporary feeling of smugness for being so clever. It's true – you do feel smarter in that instant.

Historically, we call that the *moment of clarity*. It's nothing new. The problem is, we have never been very good at getting people there in a predictable way (unless you happen to be very articulate or demonstrative). Maybe the material wasn't compelling. Maybe it was bad design. Or maybe it was you. There are a gazillion reasons why people don't quite understand what was being presented or communicated to them. And in a nutshell, that's exactly the problem. There's no one-size-fits-all solution or magic bullet to use every time to fix this. We need to rely on our own ability to figure out what makes sense to other people.

As natural communicators and storytellers, we excel at talking in person. Our goal when face-to-face is to look for some kind of positive visual feedback indicating we're on the right track with our approach (this doesn't work at all with the written word – as authors, we just choose to believe we're making sense ;-) In person, we look at body language and listen for cues to help us make in-flight corrections to land our points. We may need to adjust our approach or tactics to make that connection we're after and be sure people are getting it. Takes practice, but it's something we all do pretty well to some degree or another.

Yet, despite all our whizzy tech and big brains, producing the moment of clarity on-demand remains an elusive and somewhat mysterious achievement. The conditions for getting there vary so much from person to person, situation to situation, there doesn't seem to be a repeatable pattern. Even though we all experience these special moments continuously throughout our lives, they are far from predictable, nor are they easy to create at will. Being able to produce a message, passage, or diagram that everyone else will immediate understand is rare because our brains are wired so differently. Our hearts respond with different emotions. Our minds see only what they want. And the fact is, people are just random sometimes. Every situation differs by individual. What emotional state are you in when you're looking at this? What is your background and life experience? How deep have you been exposed to any of the information before?

As Designers (or anyone who does a lot of presentations and talks), we try our best to be clear in our communications, unless we're just going for effect or artistic merit. We often try and improve the odds by simplifying the message. It doesn't pay to make things overly complicated or try too hard for a sophisticated design.

The clearest elevator Lobby button I have ever seen. Brilliant.

Over my career, I've tried to practice what I call *radical simplification* for communication pieces, where we get rid of as many extraneous things as possible to focus on the primary messages and key aspects. An example of that is removing all color completely from a diagram or PowerPoint slide deck to reduce distractions. Try this sometime – create something entirely in black text on white backdrop, or vice versa – no color, no fancy templates, no colorful clipart. It trains you to see what's important. Then try it out on someone. Once the message resonates, add some color back in for very specific spots to emphasize something or deliver an aspect of the message more clearly. Re-test on someone. Did it help? I be willing to bet it did. This approach doesn't work for every situation, but it's a useful exercise, nonetheless.

It's a long and challenging process to get something clear enough that most people understand it right off. The truth is, getting to the moment of clarity is just hard, even for the skilled. We need a better way to get people there - and Smart Information is it.

Engineering Clarity

Given the difficultly and effort required, it's about time for us to engineer a way of getting people to the moment of clarity reliably. Been long enough. Most of us aren't that good at it anyway left to our own devices. Add to that the potential saving of how many hours, days, weeks, and even years of people's lives that could be spent on tasks (other than the highly manual and tedious job of creating effective messaging and communication). Doesn't this all seem like it could be done by the machine now? Well, it can. Turns out AI is really good at analyzing large bodies of examples to learn how to replicate successful outcomes. Great place to start.

Smart Information, powered by AI, will help get people to the moment of clarity better than any medium that's come before it, with music perhaps as the exception (we tend to be hardwired to divine emotional clarity from music). By having so many different versions of a message or piece of information available at any time, it gets easier to find the right altitude to tell the story from and medium to convey it. Quantifying the science of how to synthesize the moment of clarity is our quest now.

I've had this hypothesis for many years that we could engineer the moment of clarity if we combined talented designers, coders, data scientists, psychologists, and marketers together and focused them specifically on the issue of creating *clarity*. We talked earlier about how information will come in different forms with multiple levels of detail depending on your situation, so the trick for this group of people is figuring out which level is right for you and then how to present it as clearly as possible to get you to the moment of clarity quickly (unless you are going for a more theatrical experience where a slow reveal is more appropriate).

Clarity is easy to recognize. You just get it.

Let's start by reverse engineering the moment of clarity. By engaging from a brain science and psychological perspective first, we stay human-centric and empathetic from the beginning. Let's figure out how the wetware part of this equation works so the tech side knows what problem to solve for. Easier said than done, but there are decades of great research to mine and new techniques in brain imaging and impulse measurement to isolate the key psychological factors that contribute to finally getting to the point of understanding something clearly.

Emotions are a critically important part of crafting a clear signal

From the physical side, can we identify regions of the brain that light up when we "get it"? Can we map out a way to get there reliably and predictably? Great questions – we'll see if it is possible. On the experiential side, we're looking for a few presentation and interaction methods that reliably get us to understanding. From a tech perspective we are identifying ways to recognize clarity in the mind or body of the recipient. If it were possible to nail down the factors that directly contribute to the light bulb going on from a psychological standpoint, we could then turn our attention to the emotional – which in many ways is the more difficult subject.

Engineering an *efficient* path to clarity isn't the whole deal here – we need to consider people's **emotions** along the way. In fact, **empathy** plays a big role in our approach. Just because you know how to make something clear doesn't mean you won't offend or anger someone. It also doesn't mean you won't overly stimulate them and cause an unintended side effect.

Knowing how people are going to react given their current state of mind or recent experiences is critically important. Looking at ways to determine possible outcomes or reactions given current context (and emotional state) will help to deliver the message in the right way at this particular time. You can't expect to get the emotional side of things correct all the time because of our irrational behavior and unexpected randomness. But, we can try to show some real empathy in our engineered solutions.

Measuring Impact

When we successfully reverse engineer getting someone to the moment of clarity effectively and predictably, the next question should be "How does that compare to the old way of doing it? Did it really improve anything?" Fair question. And certainly one that engineers and researchers need to pay attention to – how do you measure the impact of this cognitive task?

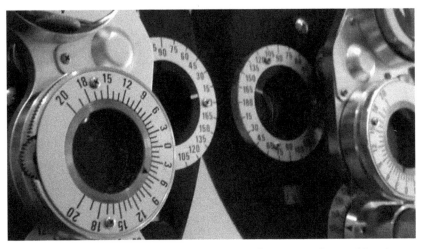

Being able to quantify the amount of impact is an experience thing too

In our case, measuring the *impact* of the moment of clarity is more than just a scientific efficiency gain, it represents a new way of approaching the experience overall. Instead of optimizing for mechanical effectiveness, we need to spend most of our effort on achieving a neural and emotional connection – very different feats. And substantially more difficult to objectively measure. Unless we have access to advanced imaging to see specific parts or pathways in the brain light up when we achieve our goal, this measurement is reliant on subjective means like standard inquiry or potentially on biometric measures like vitals and micro facial expressions using something like Microsoft Cognitive Services with cameras.

The impact to be measured is also spread across two very different task orientations – authoring and consumption. The amount of change is no less dramatic on either side of the equation – creating content that can get people to moment of clarity is a huge effort, but no bigger than finding the repeatable approaches to creating clarity on playback.

Authoring content will be hugely affected by an injection of services and platforms to create Smart Information "containers" that are capable of housing multiple representations of the same information in a multitude of forms. They also need access to on-board or Cloud-based intelligence to be contextually relevant in message delivery. That's a lot of moving parts. Measuring a change like this is a major overhaul that cannot be looked at from a purely mechanical labor perspective – it's not an apples to apples comparison with previous methods. We can now generate an exponentially larger amount of work in a fraction of the time using the machine. That alone represents a major shift and potential inflection point on the authoring side of the equation.

We are moving into a semi-autonomous or fully automated content creation age. Let that sync in for just a moment.

Consumption is equally affected by this transformational shift. A measure of "how much better" is completely subjective if we cannot figure out a quality metric that takes into account the dynamic nature of the form. We should look carefully at the satisfaction with on-the-fly forms vs. the familiar original delivered in a rigid (albeit well-known) state. Which did the job better?

Our measure for Smart Information consumption cannot focus on a single instance or instantiation of the content – it needs to be evaluated over time as a cumulative effect on understanding and satisfaction. Looking at just individual moments in time miss the bigger point. We have changed the fundamental nature of information. This is no longer about a single data point, it's about all of them, over time.

Continuous Learning

When we do crack the code and figure out how to reliably engineer the moment of clarity using Smart Information constructs, it will be critical to learn what works best for each of us individually on both the consumption and authoring sides of the equation. The system needs to **learn** what we want or need.

"Always be closing" was Alec Baldwin's famous line from the film *Glengarry Glen Ross.* Smart Information has its own version of that line – "Always be learning." The overall system uses AI to pay attention to what is working for you and what isn't, whether you are creating or consuming content. This is the same kind of AI found in your smartphone or smartwatch that pays attention to your daily commute. From your patterns, it knows that telling you it will take 43 minutes to get home is probably valuable when you start driving home from work at 5:37 PM. The system is always learning.

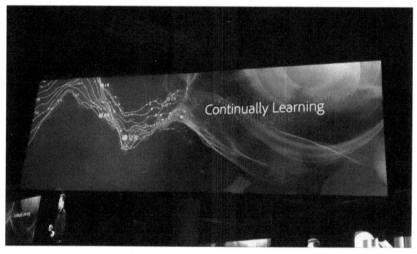

Continuous Learning is part of Adobe's new creative platform

To be specific, the type of Artificial Intelligence that we'll use to track and respond to your reactions when dealing with Smart Information is known as *Reinforcement Learning*. It's a form of Machine Learning that uses knowledge of behavioral psychology to employ software agents to maximize rewards, with the goal of creating a better experience for you. It gets signals from our choices when dealing with a particular delivery medium and form during consumption tasks to inform a "model" or learning algorithm that improves over time. The net result is a system that is paying attention to our reactions and behavior to feed them back into the initial state decisions for future interactions with similar types of information. Continuous learning cycle.

You'd never really notice if Reinforcement Learning was in play during typical consumption scenarios, just as you don't pay much attention to the prompts and notifications you get throughout your day from the smartphone. The system we build to get people to the moment of clarity needs to integrate this type of tech to achieve the very people-centric focus we have for the experiences. Some of the most advanced technology we have ever developed to address mind-bendingly complex problems will be employed regularly to solve one of the seemingly simplest of problems – how systems and devices will to talk to me so I "get it".

PART 2

THE
EXPERIENCE

THE AGE OF SMART INFORMATION

Dimensional Design

We're moving way beyond 3D. Strap in.

In a world where any piece of information or content can have multiple representations available at any time, which is the right one for me at this particular moment and situation? And how many dimensions of data do you show me at one time?

That's precisely the challenge for today's Designers of Smart Information – how do you (and the AI) know what form to use and what dimensions to represent for your audience? Well, the truth is that's a trick question. There's never just one solution that's best for everyone when it comes to understanding or communicating. It's always dependent upon the individual. Adding to the difficulty of choosing is the requirement that every representation needs to have its own intelligence to help govern its own behavior, appearance, relationships, and history. The complexity escalates quickly. And that's when the fun begins.

Multiple Dimensions

Designing for a world-ready system where we communicate the same information in multiple ways with built-in intelligence has led us to revisiting our standard approach. We will collectively need to shift our design thinking and execution efforts in two major ways – dimensionality and active assistance.

First, we need to create new forms of existing information that are **inherently multi-dimensional** (not just 3D, but rather taking into account multiple axes of evaluation such as context and audience, which may manifest in entirely new entities). And second, people will need to stop relying on manual design for everything and **embrace AI to assist** with the most appropriate arrangement and generate additional formats and levels of detail.

Both of those shifts are captured within the framework of **Dimensional Design**, an approach and methodology to dynamically work out the various forms of any digital artifact and when to appropriately surface them. This post-modern design approach uses AI to consider multiple factors within the current context to determine the best formats to create and present, taking into account the situation, preferences, behavior, and emotion of the audience. Dimensional Design utilizes the ability for AI to reason in a similar way to people when making its decisions about appropriateness.

This design direction embraces an enormous shift in the industry's expectations of what can be done with an AI to drive creation and interaction. Our everyday tasks, interactions, and relationships will profoundly change once these design techniques become solid and more widespread. The thinking required here goes well beyond appearance, to focus on behavior, intelligence, and ethics. We are at that point where we need to trust the machine.

[NOTE] **For the Designers in the room,** *Dimensional Design is not the same as Spatial Design, which primarily works out how to best integrate 3D content and holograms into the world around us using 6DoF to navigate the experience. Spatial Design generally focuses on experiences rooted in augmented reality, mixed reality, or virtual reality. Dimensional Design is much broader and not limited to those 3D-based technologies but does use Spatial Design techniques (and every other kind of design thinking) to synthesize solutions that incorporate multiple layers of content for clarity. It goes well beyond 3D.*

The important part to recognize here is the shift from a single one-dimensional original form to a multi-faceted entity. The core of Dimensional Design focuses on how to best utilize the additional dimensions to depict a particular meaning in the right way for the current context and audience, with memorable presentation and real impact. Sometimes we'll use an audio-based format, sometimes imagery, other times immersive 3D models. Not to be confused with that cheap parlor trick of showing a 3D model overlaid on top of some text, dynamically picking a representation is a very complex problem to solve in real-time.

Current Context

Smart Information artifacts need to analyze the current situation to address **content, clarity, focus, time, location, medium, altitude, delivery, format, actions,** and **emotion**. Not your usual two or three dimensions. This is a *multi-dimensional design space*. In fact, there's even more to add to the mix, including **spatial, temporal, sonic,** and **sensory-based** aspects. It takes a new kind of design thinking, literally a *high-dimensional space* approach, to figure out how this all works together seamlessly.

Contextually Relevant design here means we are analyzing the current environment to take into consideration all of these dimensions available through sensors and APIs. The AI platforms and services available to us help gather the inputs we need from physical and digital realms.

- Content
- Clarity
- Focus
- Time
- Location
- Medium

- Altitude
- Delivery
- Format
- Actions
- Emotion
- Spatial

- Temporal
- Sonic
- Sensory-based

We also need to remember that few people have done this type of design before now. If you are a Quantum physics and computing expert, maybe you have wrapped your head around this type of problem. But most of us have not been exposed to truly multi-dimensional design spaces. It's not easy. You have to keep all of these variables in your head while simultaneously remembering to keep the person who's trying to use this in mind the whole time.

Remember Mr. Spock's three-dimensional chess board from the original Star Trek? In order to play that game you needed to not only anticipate your opponent's moves in advance, but be able to plot them out for yourself in three-space to visualize the possible next gambit. This is just like that – but way harder :/

[NOTE] **For the Engineers in the room**, *this real-time analysis and processing of the environment by AI and ML does not all need to happen on the intelligent edge, but that would be optimal if enough processing and bandwidth were available. The delays in using a remote service may be negligible, but high responsiveness at the point of interaction drives much better satisfaction. That said, 5G looks promising on the bandwidth front to assist in throughput.*

The key to this type of difficult design work is to not get caught up in all the high-dimensional complexity, but rather to simplify it all down by envisioning it from the perspective of the impatient person experiencing it. Make it personal. Think about their current background, environment, time of day, location, rules, and behavior. Those all have a huge role to play in how we create the optimal way to communicate the key aspects of a digital artifact at this exact moment. It's never going to be one size fits all.

There's such a strong bias toward the familiar when it comes to working with these kind of digital objects – documents, tweets, and photos, that we have a natural aversion to change of any kind here. So, taking this gigantic leap forward is kinda like a series reboot of your favorite movie trilogy (let's say *Star Trek* for example) – there's enormous stakes, but high reward if done right. Since we're explorers, let's try it. What could go wrong?

Making Sense

Just as in the real world, we'll let our intuition, experiences, and senses guide us along the path to designing a solution. As always, we will start with people, not technology, to be our north star. All the whizzy technology, advanced capabilities, stellar features, and new-to-world functionality that Smart Information promises are nowhere near as important as how all this makes people feel and subsequently act.

Making sense of the world around us without consciously thinking about it is how we operate normally, meaning it's not something we focus on, but rather just do. In the same way, any solution that we move forward with for Smart Information should plan on making sense of the world continually by monitoring what's happening and paying attention to our audience's reactions. We'll need to feed that data back into the system for analysis and decision making. This type of constant monitoring/feedback loop could not be more natural for us to understand as humans, but it is indeed exceptionally difficult to engineer in reliable ways in software for all situations.

Artificial Intelligence is needed here to assist us with making sense of the world so quickly. There's a lot to get through, and it's of paramount important to the overall Smart Information experience that we remain very aware of our surroundings and context in order to make good decisions about form and altitude of messaging. It's what most of Dimensional Design is geared to deal with.

Monitoring and sensing of our environment can be done through any number of hardware and software mechanisms that mimic the wetware of our brains. Smartphones, smartwatches, computers, rooms, and medical implants all serve as great sources of environmental data to determine context. Not to mention how our software services and apps have recorded a long history of our interests, preferences, actions, and general patterns of behavior that can also be fed into a system to establish a "current context". Using both hardware and software as input gives us a decent picture of the situation to base decisions on. But, we'll need a new conceptual framework to think about how to deal with all this context input.

Sensory Design is an emerging language and approach we can use in this stage of the process to literally design for our senses. It was developed to analyze and determine how to react to common environmental factors with the help of Artificial Intelligence. Sensory Design looks at our sight, hearing, touch, movement, spatial awareness, and agency to determine how to best proceed with design problems like the ones we face with Smart Information. There's a natural fit here for Designers and Engineers to leverage this evolving body of work that's rooted in cognitive science and Machine Learning. And in general, look for a major shift in experience design away from traditionally silo'ed approaches to this more multi-disciplinary methodology.

To get started with Dimensional Design, let's focus on just a few aspects of being clear (which is the main point). One aspect is how the message itself is being presented, and the other aspect is the effectiveness of the medium used to deliver it.

Beautifully Clear

Perhaps the most important design aspect of Smart Information is its focus on creating clarity. Rather than focus on ways to enhance or decorate the visual appearance of something, we look for ways to be clear, regardless of form. Being clearly understood is one of the most difficult things to master in any type of communication, and differs from person to person, culture to culture, so this movement has made that a primary goal at every step. The Dimensional Design methodology puts being clear as priority one, regardless of the medium and mechanics employed to get the job done.

Clearly Beautiful

Beautifully Clear.

Don't try to be beautiful first. True beauty is clarity.

Another major part of clarity is being **inclusive**. We need to design all of our information with *everyone* in mind, not just people like ourselves. Again, easier said than done when we don't consider how many of us are differently-abled and don't experience things in exactly the same way. We create problems from the start when we don't pay attention to such a basic design requirement rooted in human decency. There are now great online guides and books on *Inclusive Design* practices that can help us be more emphatic when designing anything people could encounter during our experiences. We cannot let unconscious bias or ignorance of abilities prevent us from being as clear as possible for everyone, in any situation.

Just Tell Me

There's often too much emphasis put on the presentation aspect of what we communicate and not enough on whether it's clear to the person receiving it. We create posts and videos that take forever to get to the point. They have no sense of being direct, concise, or clear. The canonical example of this what happens all the time with corporate PowerPoint presentations. People want to impress and wow their audience, so they focus on the appearance, transitions, and cramming tons of data into a single slide in an effort to be "effective". That almost always has the exact opposite effect.

This also happens quite a bit with data visualization, where we become obsessed with using the proper type of chart or graph according to the data viz experts. That's fine of course, unless it's not actually helping people understand what the data represents. Even worse is when we use exotic looking visualizations that are "beautiful" compared to previous methods. Indeed.

Just tell me what you need to tell me. You don't need to tell me a story first. You don't need to build a case step-by-step or lead up to it slowly then hit me with the big reveal. Just tell me. I appreciate your storytelling chops, but we don't need to press those into service unless I ask for it or it's warranted, like in a good conversation.

JUST TELL ME.

Please, just tell me.

It is pretty straightforward to prioritize this once you understand how important it really is to everyday communication. People tend to use way more preamble than necessary when answering. Think about it.

High Impact

Our goal is to always be beautifully clear, but honestly it doesn't hurt to be clearly beautiful while doing it ;-)

The best way to communicate something effectively is to be memorable in some significant way. We have an abundance of methods with Dimensional Design to do just that. Many of them have to do with the manner in which the information is presented. We can start with just our voice, move to a simple textual summary, illustrate it with images or diagrams, project holograms into the air, or bring you into an immersive virtual world. The possibilities seem unlimited, and each in their own way are exceptionally impactful when used to their best advantage.

The packaging and format that something comes in can help determine its ability to have high impact and be remembered by people. If I tell you that I'm not at all interested in reading comic books, you would be wise to not try and teach me something I need to remember in that format. It won't keep my interest long enough to be memorable. But, if you show me the same thing in a thirty second video, all of a sudden, I could repeat back to you exactly what happened along with the dialogue. Format influences impact.

We are now at the point with our presentation technologies and formats that we can be stunningly high impact on-demand (when used responsibly). We have achieved photorealism in our movie special effects and regularly conjure up imagery that has never existed. We're bound only by our imaginations when it comes to finding ways to be impactful to the people who are interested.

I like to call this presentation impact the "Transformer effect" of Smart Information. In the movie series, there are a set of cars and trucks that literally transform themselves from somewhat ordinary looking vehicles into awesome three story tall warrior robots. Watching them morph into these metal creatures is truly something to behold, as too is the conversion of ordinary text into impactful new forms for us. It's also surprisingly comforting to observe that same element returning to its quiet resting state.

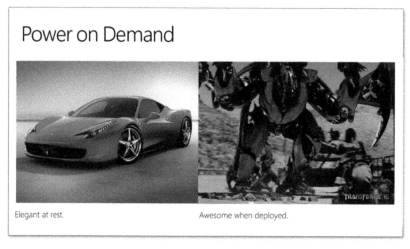

Power on Demand

Elegant at rest.

Awesome when deployed.

Smart Information is just like a Transformer (credit: Ferrari, Paramount)

The Spatial Computing aspects of Smart Information are what set it apart from any previous medium of communicating. As I described in my book *Envisioning Holograms*, there's something primordial and hardwired about our fascination with digital ghosts in our world. We can't help but be transfixed by them and want to engage. It's that natural attraction that cements the relationship between Spatial and Smart Information. We want people to more deeply explore. Presenting information in Mixed Reality is a highly effective way to do that.

Let's take full advantage of that magical relationship.

Ambient Intelligence

What happens when everything is a know-it-all?

Asking your Amazon Alexa to play a song is one thing – but being able to ask that song itself what it's about is quite another.

The day is coming quickly when anything and everything will be able to respond to your questions and even have a conversation with you about the things most relevant to itself. That includes events that happened during its creation, like in the example of a song knowing what inspired a musician to write it. Whether we're talking about a document from your manager or a video of your favorite band, the digital artifacts we encounter each day will have enough intelligence to tell their own stories. They will be more than rigid containers for static data. Most will converse with us, answer our questions, and maybe even ask us things if we let them.

Our world is changing so rapidly, it's hard to imagine how we could be shocked by anything these days. But this is different. "Things" don't historically talk with us or allow us to query them about anything and everything having to do with themselves, related objects, and people. Now they do, thanks to the combination of Artificial Intelligence, Spatial Computing, and a whole bunch of clever people around the world.

Brains Onboard

The base design for Smart Information calls for AI to be used to help enable two very particular features – (1) the ability to dynamically figure out what the best representation of something is, and (2) enabling any digital artifact to be queried, conversed with, or deeply explored through an interactive exchange.

How long until everything wants to talk with you?

This ability to converse with us is nothing new for devices and services that employ Artificial Intelligence to recognize voice input. The difference here is that by using Machine Learning to analyze and prepare responses, and Reinforcement Learning to refine our interaction with individual people, we have created the opportunity for *any* digital artifact to act like our Amazon Alexa and answer questions. And it feels like it's holding a genuine conversation with us the whole time.

Engineering-wise, the way we enable this feat is to have either the digital artifact (i.e. information) connect with an online service in the Cloud to process the requests and respond appropriately, or conversely, we can do the processing on what's referred to as the "intelligent edge" (meaning, on the local device). The implications of this are super interesting, as it can seem to the person having the conversation they are in fact talking with an intelligent piece of information. That's startling to consider. We're just getting used to "things" talking with us, never mind our digital artifacts. Smart Information makes this commonplace.

The way in which this on-board intelligence decides to engage with us has much to do with crowd-sourced patterns that have been analyzed, but more to do with the individual's behavior and actions over time. We are entering a time when you are truly understood by the machine.

There is also the ability for Smart Information objects to do **computation**, **calculation**, and **simulation** by leveraging external services or internal code. This comes in handy when you need it to play what-if simulations or project scenarios forward based on a specific set of variable values. Imagine being able to inquire directly to the asking price text of a home itself what the mortgage and down payments would be. Tomorrow's calculators and configurators are hidden within our most common information forms today - text.

Pivotal Decisions

A key part of the intelligence applied to Smart Information is its ability to choose the right form of information to present (audio, photo, video, haptic, etc.) for a given situation. That's always a pivotal decision in the communication process. It's also one of the determining factors for whether we are being clear or not. Getting these decisions right consistently has everything to do with how "good" this system is considered to be over time. Making a solid connection while communicating goes a long way.

We can't afford to get this initial decision of what to present wrong – but we will. Our efforts here will certainly improve over time with the help of Machine Learning on the backend and Reinforcement Learning on the frontend, but to start there will be a lot of experimentation on form. So, for now let's focus our built-in intelligence on solving for the right thing - clarity. In order to do that, we have several basic questions to run through each time.

Who? Just like any decision made about how to communicate effectively, we should start by evaluating who is listening or paying attention. Do we know anything about them? If so, what specifically can we use to establish a connection to engage them early? In a Smart Information system, you potentially have secure access to a great deal of approved background on the person or audience to be sorted through. Our goal here is to customize and personalize our initial form to feel exactly right for its target. The digital object will know that I prefer summaries and brief overviews rather than someone like you who might like more detail by default.

Why? Every experience design opportunity should start with asking the obvious question – Why are we doing this? In this case, knowing what the person is doing currently (i.e. walking down the street) helps us to understand the context of why they may be asking a particular question or requesting certain information. That helps the AI connect the dots to infer potential scenarios.

In many common cases, it will be completely obvious why this information was asked for – it's the answer to a direct question. Other times it will be somewhat mysterious, with lots of room for error in interpreting. That's where great design comes in – being ready to ask a clarifying question, pivot into a new format, show a different level of detail, or even time shift some aspect of the interaction to make it easier to answer. I asked for directions to that restaurant when I was at work to see how long it would take to get there, but now that I'm on my way I'm much more interested in some landmarks along the way to help me find the place. The question remained the same – the answer should have morphed over time to fit the circumstances.

When? The exact time something is being asked for will determine a great deal about the form of the answer. If we are being asked to synthesize an answer and generate various levels of detail right now, we'll use the current context to govern that process. If it's clear the information will not be used now but at some later time or date, we'll have to take our best shot at what will be needed and be ready to reevaluate when the request is updated. Changing an answer's form based on time shifting is a feature of Smart Information that allows for a more appropriate level of detail. Time is an incredibly important trigger for appropriateness. A game's score is of little use if it isn't updated each time it's being looked at.

Where? Exactly where in the world you'll be using this piece of Smart Information governs its appearance, sound, format, and behavior (just to name a few). This goes deeper than localizing or translating a piece of content dynamically. Information really could be quite different depending on exactly where you author or consume it. Locale dictates special considerations around social norms and customs that apply nowhere else. Once we develop more advanced authoring tools and delivery platforms, something like this book could be initially created in English only, but then be translated during a post-process into a German version, or again at runtime as a Spanish audio book. This ability for AIs to do on-the-fly language translation is already available and working.

How? Personal preference plays the biggest role in how a given piece of information should be delivered. This is the primary differentiator for Smart Information – it has the ability to morph information into whatever form is most appropriate given all the factors we evaluate. For example, we normally expect tweets, documents, mail, etc.in some visual form because they are dealt with on screens. But, if the system knows you are accessing them via voice commands in the car, or your smartwatch when running, you may get an audio version of them automatically. At the office or school when you have access to large spaces with high quality projection, perhaps you'll get a room full of holograms.

What? Once we know who is asking and why this information was requested, it gets a bit easier to figure out what form and level of detail is called for. In some ways, this calculation of what to present after those previous questions have been answered is the easiest of all. It's a straightforward mapping into the right object and altitude to be presented in if this is computed at the end of the process. For example, if you are casually browsing your social media feed on a Sunday morning, you will probably get mostly video content (the level of detail you most often use when you are not pressed for time) while using your tablet based on your past behavior and the fact that the information "knows you". That said, this is the part of the equation we will get wrong many times along the way to developing a dependable and predictable system. People are so fickle and nuanced, sometimes you just can't win.

And finally, **How Much?** When pivoting to the right solution for your context, it may require one or more versions of something to be generated that have not ever been produced manually. That's where the value of this approach really shines. We'll get the AI machinery to do a lot of the heavy lifting for that content creation, but there is a cost. It may be incremental or micro transactional – still, we should be aware of creating new work that deserves to be compensated. We shouldn't use this new system as an excuse to build out ridiculously complex and expensive content solutions that create friction for consumers. We need to enable AIs to use good judgement when looking at what should be provided as default forms of something with little to no cost. Just because we want to be complete, it's not always financially responsible to do so for the intended audience in their current context.

Best Behavior

Of all the changes that Smart Information has brought to our text and images, the most dramatic departure from past forms is feeling like our information artifacts now have a personality and unique set of behavioral traits all of their own. Smart Information objects respond like they're alive and behave as if they genuinely want to be interacted with. It often feels like they are proactively inviting a conversation and deeper exploration.

As we have all learned throughout our own lives, behavior is something we need to pay attention to now or pay the consequences for later. Few things could be worse than something coming to life, only to be misbehaved from the start.

People like when things are predictable, especially when it comes to someone's behavior and manners (and yes, content does have manners now). It can be as subtle as knowing your coworker is going to keep it PG-rated while at work even though you may have saltier talks on the same subject at the pub. In a similar way, knowing that Smart Information will dependably present the most appropriate level of detail for the current situation assures you the boss won't be disappointed by your last minute presentation during a hastily called 5pm meeting.

Feeling like any piece of data or information has the ability to be queried, interrogated, or messed with is a big behavioral change in the history of computing. It's almost as if we transplanted the capabilities of an Alexa, Cortana, or Siri into each and every digital artifact we come into content with. Many of them are never used in that way, but pretty amazing that any of them could, at any time, in any situation, and be on their best behavior.

Remember Now?

As all of our digital artifacts start to respond to us, and we back to them, there's a need to remember those interactions and build a detailed history of what's transpired to help inform and govern future engagements. You don't want to feel as if your extremely important quarterly sales report doesn't remember a thing about you telling it how to respond to questions about last quarter's shortfall to your boss's boss.

In an era of everything around us, whether physical or digital, having some degree of intelligence, we'll come to depend upon the ambient environment recognizing us and our information. Just like your doorman remembers chatting with you when strolling in with that pizza at 2am last night, your information will also recall the last set of interactions it had with you and be able to pick up where you left off in a way that feels appropriate.

Much of that remembering, adjusting, and compensating will be taken care of for us by a constant monitoring and educational process known as Reinforcement Learning (RL). Part of the Machine Learning branch of AI, these RL algorithms help inform decisions about interactions based on our history with these objects.

Never fear, the machine will be paying close attention so that you'll feel like it's somewhat intelligent (that is, for a well-behaved know-it-all ;-)

Experiential Ethics

Micro-Decisions on Macro Issues

Is that tweet a lie? Did that email request go too far? Did you mean to purposely offend people in that presentation? You do know that could be considered theft, right?

It's frightening how many ethical questions arise but remain unasked and unanswered when we are creating and consuming digital content. It's not until we interact with other people that they come into the light and become something to be discussed or dealt with. Because there isn't anyone else standing over our shoulder monitoring us while we go about our business, our unconscious biases and bad behavior make their way into our communication. Much of it unintentional, and avoidable. Yet, most of us would object to any kind of monitoring that flagged "questionable" items or ethical grey areas.

Who are you (computer) to tell me what not to do or say? It's a fair point. Our Artificial Intelligence powered digital assistants are just following their programming and whatever ethics (if any) were put into their model or rules. They are not always right, nor are they smarter than us. But, when designing a new worldwide system of content authoring and consumption, you've gotta ask yourself if you can live with the consequences of not having that kind of discussion first, as painful as it may be.

Information has always been used for both good and well let's just say more nefarious reasons. We are left to figure out which one for ourselves too many times a day to keep track of. Some of us are evolved enough to not allow surface level attributes to bias our thinking about a topic without knowing more, while others are impulsive and quick to judge. That's human nature. Some people's reaction to certain topics are thoughtful and measured, while others choose to accept new information at face value and don't care to dig any deeper.

The commonality among all of these different reactions is they are all triggered by some degree on first impressions. It's natural. We may think something is reputable just because of who or what is saying it. How it looks. What visuals accompany the message. Where it is presented? How forcefully? Was it said respectfully or full of anger?

The beauty we seek is not found in first impressions,
but rather in how the truth reveals itself.

The systems we create to enable powerful new information experiences should understand how influential they can be at first impression and strive to engage people in a deeper exploration of the related data and topics in order for them to more fully understand and form their own ideas of the truth. The skillful way these additional aspects are revealed to us over time often become critical to the challenge of providing people with more than a surface level view of their information.

Ethical Design

We have an obligation and responsibility as designers of this new communication medium and its related technologies to do the right thing – strive to be ethical and moral in our words and actions. The creation of first impressions is not the only area that needs special attention, but it is an important one. The impressions that result from receiving any new bit of created information can now be so easily manipulated to elicit specific responses, we need to examine how any new system will add to that problem or put mechanisms in place to illuminate when it's happening. Persuasion is key.

Beware of highly persuasive info masquerading as Pandas and Cats

Persuasion used to be something that was practiced deftly (but not continually) by the charismatic among us – now it's been weaponized and used regularly to bludgeon our general perception through continual targeted messaging. We need to acknowledge these information warfare effects are real and take the appropriate action to educate and allow for choice in the both the creation and consumption of Smart Information.

We need look no further than the Advertising industry for great examples of using ethical design well and where it has completely failed us. Skilled advertisers (with different end goals in mind) have always had the ability to manipulate public opinion and elicit action. The modern communication tools and technologies we have been using for the last several years have amplified that effect to dangerous levels. We're just now realizing now how deeply the ability to effectively influence people through targeted information has made its way into common artifacts like Facebook posts and Instagram videos.

People are certainly more aware of that kind of manipulation today than in the past (with Gen Z being almost immune to traditional advertising). In fact, we can learn so much from that generation about not letting our superficial analysis form a first impression that drives our lasting impression, without first doing additional digging or sanity checking. This is precisely where the multi-faceted capabilities of Smart Information can help. Layers and layers of additional data and related tidbits are available at any time, making deep exploration simple if you want it. Remember with Smart Information there's always more than meets the eye.

Micro-Decisions

Some of the most important decisions we'll make in the near future are related to how much we want to purposely influence vs. trying to be objective in the way we communicate. Just as we have built-in spellchecking and grammar analysis today, tomorrow's apps, platforms, and toolsets used to convey information to each other will have the ability to monitor **tone**, **accuracy**, **factualness**, **timeliness**, **offensiveness**, and **persuasiveness** of content.

The same is true of how information is received – what was your **reaction**, **emotion**, and subsequent **action**. It's truly going to be a *Brave New World* if we don't get a handle on the intention and use of these capabilities early on in the adoption process.

To evaluate the tone or intent of a message you are sending, or conversely, information you are consuming, the systems will use a variety of techniques to analyze the "sound" of the speaking voice, intonation, inuendo, humor, darkness, slang, encoding, and history of similar communiques. We'll even pull data from hardware sensors, cameras, and microphones for additional cues to your emotional state. Heartrate informs emotion, facial micro ticks indicate stress, voice inflections hint at intent, etc. Once the analysis is done by the AI, trends and patterns will be considered and the result fed back into active Machine Learning models to enhance the overall effectiveness of the larger system serving the ecosystem. The net result is that we learn more about the subtleties of information creation and consumption in a data-driven way. That leads to improvements on both sides of the equation (creation and consumption), and of course could lead to misuse and abuse if not proactively looked for and compensated for.

Once we can effectively understand the underlying intent, structure, and emotion of information it will be time to turn our attention to how we can further improve our understanding of it through a series of AI-driven **micro-decisions** in the authoring pipeline and also the consumption and sharing side. This may appear to be like the "red squiggle" you find underneath any misspelled words today. We already alert you to grammar issues and make suggestions. Layering additional dimensions such as emotional impact, persuasion, and accuracy could easily be envisioned as a normal part of creating or editing.

These micro-decisions affect things like if you will continue authoring a Tweet that was flagged as looking offensive to the AI, or if your news feed automatically hides certain news stories about political figures because you have been emotionally affected by them in the past. This is the part of the movie where everyone realizes the human-like AI has gotten out of control. It's not usually that dramatic in real life, but there is cause for concern when your tools are telling you not to send that mail so quickly, or you were being a little harsh on your brother in that text message.

It's incredibly exciting to imagine this type of AI-assisted workflow behaving well and being genuinely helpful. It's also equally frightening to imagine micro-censoring of content and touchy decisions being made on your behalf without directly consulting you. I'll give a slightly ridiculous example to make a point – imagine if your hammer delivered an electric shock just enough to make you drop it because it thought you were doing a really bad job of nailing things in today, and you're probably not going to do any better this time. Indeed.

The question isn't whether this will all happen on a widespread basis, but rather *when* it will happen exactly. All the tech exists now, and our best data scientists and software engineers are already working on it. So, there's no need to debate the *if*, it's the how will we deal with these potentially disruptive innovations coming into our everyday lives. If history is any teacher, the answer is poorly. Our fundamental nature is good, but our actions not so much. We need to consider the bigger picture here – the macro consequences of our actions or inactions. Will a trillion AI-powered micro-decisions a minute about our information cause an unintended worldwide societal change that we don't see coming? Perhaps. It's that type of issue we should consider as we invent and build these Smart Information systems.

"With great power comes great responsibility."

Trust Issues

Even being a tiny bit mindful of questionable ethics and the dark side of automation and intelligence-powered distribution systems is enough to make you realize we need some checks and balances as we move forward. There are a few obvious ways that decisions will be integrated into the content pipeline – autopilot, assisted, and manual.

Autopilot is a good metaphor to use when describing the type of Smart Information experiences that don't require any direct input during authoring or playback to "shape" the information. AI makes decisions all along the content pipeline on our behalf, based on well-understood patterns and templates. Automated agents are then used to gather, analyze, and package up the content and levels of detail. There have been many examples of news stories and sports recaps being written and published without any human input required. These stories are monitored of course, and could have been manually overridden to correct mistakes or unfortunate word choices or puns that are a bit too subtle for the AI to catch at the moment.

You could also imagine this type of autopilot process being completely unattended for well-understood material, but there should always be a mechanism for examining or pausing at any stage, as well as pausing and putting a person back in charge. This is what happens today with self-driving cars. The person sitting in the vehicle can and should take control if they need to, but it's usually a smooth ride.

As we push our capabilities to the "intelligent edge", the interesting part of autopilot mode is the amount of micro-decisions that could be made on our behalf about tuning many of the variable factors we discussed earlier – persuasion, emotional impact, accuracy, etc. These systems take both our history and current context into account when deciding what to share with us. The decision-making models for these tools and systems will need to be trained with our established ethics policies in place and our moral compass turned on. We cannot unleash a worldwide content creation system on autopilot with no conscience.

Manual decision-making requires a single person, group, or even "trusted" AI, to be responsible throughout the entire process of creating, sharing, or consuming information – which is for the most part today's operating model. Our tools are geared toward manual authoring with some basic assists and services available on demand. The person always stays in control. This is where most but not all the bad behavior happens, unintended or otherwise. The good news is we can control this, regardless of outcome.

Assisted is the blend of both those two models for information creation and consumption. The system can help you when you ask for or perhaps look like you need it. The big difference with this model is that every decision point in the process will be augmented in some non-trivial way by technology or other people to help achieve the best result. Just as my spell checker is watching every character I type to see when words are incorrectly formed, our background Machine Learning services will be watching and learning, ready to invoke an AI agent to assist you with decisions, big and small, straightforward or controversial. They'll tell you when you're offending without realizing it, hurting someone's feelings by accident, or purposely just being a jerk.

Even activities as simple as reading a book or watching the latest video can be "assisted" more proactively when we employ Reinforcement Learning agents to observe what works best for you in hopes of presenting it that way. The ethics and behavioral assist come in the form of what type of information and level of detail suits your current situation. Will showing you the opposition viewpoint on a hot topic help you be a bit more empathetic to those ideas or will it just piss you off? This assisted approach will be the first stop on our journey to the autopiloted future.

"Use your head, but have a heart."

PART 3

THE
SYSTEM

THE AGE OF SMART INFORMATION

Information Objects

We're gonna need somewhere to put all this

Up to now, we've mostly talked about why Smart Information emerged, what is does for us, and how it behaves. Now it's time to chat about the underlying technical structure that makes it all possible – *Information Objects*.

Smart Information should be thought of as an entire system, not just a single technology or construct. It may be nothing special compared to other recent whizzy innovations from an architecture and deployment standpoint, but this system does have a unique set of capabilities on the Design and interaction side (which we'll get into shortly). For now, let's talk about how this rich functionality is encapsulated within a single representation, much like HTML can act as both a content framework and markup language for everything on the web. It's more complicated than that, but a fine place to start the conversation is with a ubiquitous standard.

We should start with digging into how these ultra-modern containers of information are represented behind-the-scenes from a technology perspective and what they are capable of doing for us experientially within the Smart Information ecosystem.

[NOTE] For the Non-Engineers in the room, *sorry but this next part has a bit of technical mumbo jumbo mixed in to make some key points to the technical crowd. Will try to keep it to a minimum. Stay with me.*

New Construct

The digital containers for any content elements found within the Smart Information universe are called *Information Objects*. They are the base construct for definitions, interaction, queries, and interop. Think of Information Objects as framing of a house – it holds all of the other elements together, but does not dictate exactly how those elements look, act, or behave. From an engineering perspective, Smart Objects are similar to the HTML markup representation of a web page. It's a human readable, easy to parse, and lightweight definition of a fairly complex object. It's expected that Information Objects will eventually become a native element on the web and consumed by HTML browsers.

The most interesting part of Information Objects is their ability to not only define the content they represent, but also the behavior, and continuous learning aspects. Unlike an image format such as JPEG that describes its contents as some metadata followed by the bits of the picture itself, Information Objects have many different levels and layers of sub-objects and associated functionality linked to from within the markup. In many ways, it is based on the **Object-Oriented programming** models of the late 1980's, where individual objects and classes were intended to be reusable modules that were interchangeable between different code bases. Same logic and approach can be applied here with Information Objects.

Individual objects know how to create themselves, draw themselves, respond to queries and messages, and can be reused if written well.

Also, conceptually an Information Object refers to a single piece of content versus a collection, but that view can be a bit blurred if you consider a textbook a single entity instead of a collection of pages. Regardless of its underlying data, information can be as shallow or deep as you need it to be. Not every level of detail will have associated data entries in the object itself – some will be auto-generated at playback time.

Container Elements

The Information Object is an umbrella container with three major compartments – **Data**, **Representation**, and **Action**. Each of these can have both content and code (or associated services to provide the functionality), and are used to instantiate itself, react to inquiry, present itself, and tell its part of the story. Together, they form a single base unit for any type of Smart Information.

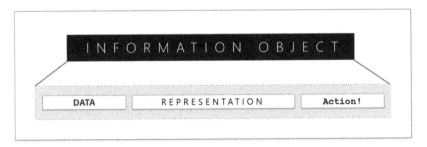

There are three main elements of an Information Object

Data

The structural element of the Information Object container that holds whatever content is associated with it is referred to generally as Data. The inline or referenced payload could be text, images, numbers, the contents of files, tweets, an entire document, music album, video, data sets, or individual data points – it's completely unconstrained. Being open and flexible on the contents enables this to scale up and across many unforeseen uses. It is intended that all of the sub-elements are infinitely expandable (practically speaking).

The Data element also wraps existing content in a loosely bound manner, making it possible to keep these containers relatively small and efficient (much like an HTML or JSON file can refer to external entities rather than using inline data which can create large file sizes and excessive load times. The Data contents can be safely manipulated and operated on through code from services and their associated models to complete particular tasks. The AI functions of **Machine Learning**, **Deep Learning**, and **Reinforcement Learning** can be used to enhance the existing Data representations in the background or on-demand.

As an example, let's say the content of this book is being stored within an object's Data element. It could be analyzed by a background Machine Learning algorithm to discover patterns of language particular to this author or translate the book content into multiple languages that preserve the author's cadence before they are ever asked for. Deep Learning functions could generate new diagrams based on text-only passages, or Reinforcement Learning can be employed to create a personalized view of the book data for the person consuming it based on their historical behavior when reading books like this one.

Representation

The element that represents how the information is conveyed to you for the current context and your personal preferences is Form. It is both the physical embodiment of the content using different mediums, and also the code that controls how that plays out. Our information can have so many different shapes, sizes, languages, sounds, and interaction models this part of the Information Object is a sophisticated one. Each of the available forms the Information Object takes have their own code for interactions specific to that medium, which are monitored and updated over time.

Taking its cues from your situation, environment, and history, the Representation is dynamically computed and pulled from available representations within the Information Object's definition. If an appropriate form is not found, one can be auto-generated depending upon its complexity and resource requirements.

For example, if your manager asks you about the latest sales numbers for this month but you're out on a morning run, you could ask your digital assistant to fetch those and read them so you don't have to stop exercising. Audio works better for that situation and is perfectly fine with you. It's easy to convey the key parts of the information to you and then back to your manager. If you had been at the office when the request came in, the same Information Object would serve up a simple chart with the data to show on a screen. If it noticed you were in a conference room with Spatial Computing devices, it could generate an **Augmented Reality**, **Mixed Reality**, or **Virtual Reality** version of the data, making it available for immersive exploration.

The Representation is fit to the situation, not the other way around – meaning we should no longer have to conform to the machine in order to get needed info.

Action

Finally, the structural element that learns how you may want to deal with this Information Object over time is Action. It uses the type of AI called Reinforcement Learning to adapt its presentation and behavior based on how you have responded to prior instances in particular situations. Not just governing behavior, Action also provides all of the standard actions you expect. From an object perspective, those include common functions such as creating, accessing, deleting, editing, sharing, duplicating, etc. Those **object-level operations** behave as you would expect them to in normal operation.

In addition, the Action may assist with making a decision or choosing not to act on what you have learned. These Actions take into account the way you like to deal with this type of information and how you may want to respond or react. The Information Object's **Emotional Intelligence** (EQ) lives here and is informed by your own actions and behavior, as well as previous incarnations across the ecosystem. The network effort of crowd sourcing and learning enhances the Action's EQ more quickly than standalone or private instances. This is where personality develops over time.

You can imagine that a social media post you create may unintentionally offend a particular party because of some language you have used. The EQ part of the Action element would flag that as you were composing it and suggest this might be the case. Or conversely, if you received a message like that in your social feed, the Information Object's own EQ may recognize you are not receptive or react poorly to messages like this and choose to file it in a place where you can view it intentionally, not blindly as part of your data river.

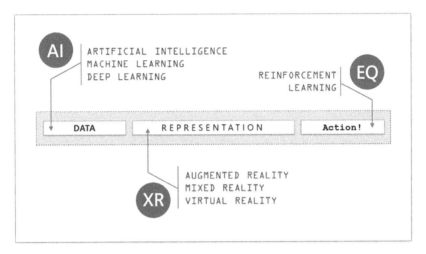

The key elements of an Information Object

Inverted Model

There is an entire universe of unique capabilities found within Smart Information. Many of those special abilities reside entirely within the Information Object construct itself, making this entity unusually capable vs. relying on the hosting app or service to provide functionality. It may seem no different for ordinary people, but for System Architects and Designers, it's a way different mental model to work with, because the object is self-sufficient and does not require a host application or service to provide its capabilities. Today, most artifact creators decide for themselves how a text passage should look and what can be done to it. With Smart Information, the current model is completely inverted. It's now the text itself that decides how it will appear (or not) and offer up capabilities of its own choosing.

---

*Smart Information uses an **inverted model** where content itself knows how to respond, instead of the hosting app or service controlling it.*

For example, the Smart Information form of a photo file would know how to present itself on whatever device its being viewed with. The apps and services being used to view it don't need to have all of the advanced capabilities built in – the photo itself knows where it's being shown and how to best present its content. There could be recorded voice commentary that is only heard when speakers are available, HDR color only shown on capable screens, location and other metadata attributes only divulged when asked about, etc. The object knows best in this model, not the hosting entity.

The implications of this are far reaching. From an architectural perspective, this isn't a novel or new approach in the world of software development – many software projects have tried to employ "smart objects" that know how to operate independently of any hosting app or service. But, in this context we are pushing down functionality into the Information Object itself (text, for example). That particular implementation is novel for now and worthy of many experiments. It's a point that we should make in a different way – this combination of AI and Spatial Computing is happening already, but what is just starting is the focus on using an object-oriented programming approach to create self-aware independent objects.

Advanced Capabilities

Smart Information is not omniscient or all encompassing, but it is a significant step toward being a self-contained and self-sufficient technological advance in the areas it serves. Information can now behave so differently than we ever imagined, it has caused us to rethink our relationships with it. Just as we have come to consider our digital assistants somewhat "aware" (much more than just software and wires), so too are our most common digital artifacts evolving into a new kind of standing with us. They feel alive.

The reason for that surprising feeling of attentiveness and flexibility is directly due to the effort put into building out its unique set of features and capabilities. With so many sophisticated things that Smart Information objects can do by themselves, it's a wonder they even exist. Until recently, this kind of self-contained, self-sufficient object would have been evaluated as way too expensive to build, debug, and maintain. That changed thanks to huge advances in AI-powered services and online architectures that allow for a mix-and-match approach to assembling features.

By combining several unrelated features within a flexible container architecture, we have created something entirely new and unprecedented in the communication realm. These new objects are responsible for truly remarkable experiences.

Multiple Representations are what give Information Objects their incredible flexibility. This luxury was only possible before now if you created them all manually yourself. Now anything can be represented in multiple forms, from the very simple (a textual summary or audio description) to the incredibly complex (such as a multi-dimensional holographic experience). And best of all, many of these new forms or representations can be dynamically-generated by the object itself using available AI services.

For any given piece of information, in addition to its native representation (the original form) and an Accessible form (Braille or high contrast for low vision), you would expect to find any or all of the following common representations:

▶ Text
▶ Audio
▶ Images/Diagrams
▶ Video
▶ Soundtrack
▶ Performance
▶ Augmented Reality
▶ Mixed Reality (Spatial or Holographic)
▶ Virtual Reality
▶ Multi-Dimensional (combination of any/all above)

These representations could be auto-generated with an AI assist, or manually created as a preferred alternative. Both have their advantages and unique properties. For now, let's say that people still have the edge here ;-)

Levels of Detail are multiple forms of the same information that allow people to consume and experience information at the right altitude for their current context and preference. Some people only ever want a short summary (like a headline) while other prefer to get all the detail right away (a spreadsheet full of data vs. a chart), and everything in-between.

Here are the common Levels of Detail for information, moving from the highest level to lowest:

▸ Meta
▸ Compact
▸ Summary
▸ Key Details
▸ Common Form
▸ Structure
▸ Objects
▸ Data

Meta is simply the high-level metadata or list of keywords that describes the essence of the object. **Compact** is a set of short phrases or small subsections that capture important elements. **Summary** is a relatively short narrative that relays the overall impression succinctly in whatever form is required. **Details** are callouts of specific parts, such as sub-elements like images and links. **Common Form** refers to the original representation at whatever level of detail it was created at. **Structure** starts to dig into the detail by revealing the framework the information is using to hold its elements together. **Objects** are individual constructs or entities that you can identify within the information such as images, text, sounds, etc. **Data** is a broad category of foundational source detail that is drawn from to shape each representation.

The representation used for a particular level is generally of the same type as its related levels. For example, if someone prefers to get their information in audio form, each successive level of detail will be more complete when moving from high-level overview to detailed and comprehensive. That said, if warranted, it's also possible for Levels of Detail to be quite a different from each other in a related collection. That's part of what the AI does for the Information Object, optimally tune each Level of Detail for the person or group consuming it.

Enhanced Interaction means we have designed-in the ability to be natively multi-modal. Rather than needing to pay attention to only one input mechanism at a time, we can now work with different input methods concurrently. You can be talking with the object while gesturing at the same time for additional tasks. This seems obvious, but most systems have not been designed to take advantage of multiple inputs at once (because its hard).

Some of the basic input types that can be combined:

- Voice
- Touch
- Gesture
- Gaze
- Haptics
- Mouse/Keyboard
- Brain Interface
- Programmatic

This type of multi-model interaction is how we deal with other people. It's a natural fit for the conversational interaction we're trying to accomplish with Smart Information.

Contextually Relevant means we are analyzing the current environment to take into consideration all of these dimensions available through sensors and APIs.

- Content
- Clarity
- Focus
- Time
- Location
- Medium
- Altitude
- Delivery

- ▶ Format
- ▶ Actions
- ▶ Emotion
- ▶ Spatial

- ▶ Temporal
- ▶ Sonic
- ▶ Sensory-based

All of these different dimensions are potentially important to the Information Object and should be handled as appropriate.

Autonomous Storytelling is the ability for any Information Object to use a narrative to tell its own story. If you ask an object "what are you?" for example, you'll get either a short summary or a lengthy description (depending on your context). This is game changing from an experiential standpoint. We are finally getting used to talking to our phone's digital assistant to carry out specific tasks like dialing or looking up something, but we aren't quite in the habit of asking a piece of information for more details.

An example of that would be seeing a news article about a controversial decision and being able to ask it directly what contributed to this happening (something we would do with another person, but not a newspaper or online news service).

Storytelling with these objects is by no means one way. We want to encourage a back and forth, just like in person. Getting to a general conversational interface with our most common types of communication artifacts is what we are striving for with Smart Information. Converting our artifacts from passive containers of information to highly interactive entities that can both tell their own story and be questioned in a conversational manner will transform the way we communicate forever.

Interoperability is one of the most important aspects of the Smart Information architecture. Being able to programmatically interact with the contents and functions of objects is invaluable in creating a worldwide ecosystem of sharing and reuse. The key idea with interop is that each Information Object can respond when queried about its contents, capabilities, and functionality. If you need to know what I think about Smart Information, just ask my book's Information Object – it'll have the ability to tell you, if I enabled that level of sharing in my security and privacy controls.

Information Objects asking other objects for access to their data, explanations, or providing context is something that could grow at a pace and scale we can't even imagine today. It's similar to the Internet of Things (IoT) projections where every sensor coming online after a certain date will all be addressable and phoning home with usage data. Except in our case, every piece of digital information created could potentially be queried or conversed with by some unfathomable amount of other objects.

Mashups and Remixes are also part of the foundational actions you should expect from Information Objects. Being able to take an entire object and combine it with others to create whole new entities is a prime use case for these constructs. Similarly, extracting sub-parts to remix into an alternate version or new creation is just as desirable and valuable. When we start creating new pieces of information with the intent of them being shared and recombined in new ways right from the beginning, we have fundamentally transformed our communication capabilities. Just imagine what's possible given permission to experiment from the author.

Information Objects make all of those breakthrough capabilities possible. Design them well.

Advanced Technology

It's getting harder to distinguish magic from tech

True breakthroughs happen suddenly, appearing out of nowhere, yet seem ridiculously logical once you see them. "Oh, of course it should work like that" is often the refrain. Giant leaps forward are never that easily achieved in reality, though. They are in the end a result of hard work, insight, and great timing. Often, they are the direct outcome of a confluence of key factors. And so it is with Smart Information.

When you see the title of a best-selling book in a review post suddenly morph itself into the physical book and then spread itself out across the space in front of you to reveal its most commented on pages, it almost seems completely normal. I mean, why would that surprise anyone these days, right? And on it goes.

Thanks to the combination of three emerging technologies (AI, Spatial Computing, and 5G) plus some enlightened experience design, our most basic communication artifacts are now our most advanced, and sometimes indistinguishable from magic.

Auto-generated Creativity

With so much experimentation around creating AI-generated art, news articles, papers, paintings, and even songs, it was just a matter of time until some turned out well. There is still so much potential for creating content that doesn't require the cleverness or irrationality of people. These types of pieces are well-defined and repeatable, requiring guidelines of course, but attainable with a high degree of confidence. Sports box scores, weather reports, financial transaction records, etc.

Will our AI agents start doing their own Envisioning sessions?

The real win for Smart Information is when our AI agents start to branch out and get creative. Not something we generally think of going well (as many of the earlier experiments with creative mediums were entertaining, but disturbingly terrible), yet it is the biggest challenge in many ways for this new AI age. We can "teach" our agents to try being creative when writing that sports article so everything is not just factual. But, there are insights and gags that only an experience sports writer would think of right now that would be missing. Not too hard to imagine we could learn and model that perspective over time with a big enough sample size. It's the nuance perhaps that will always escape an AI. That's what makes us people after all. That intangible human quality of being completely brilliant, devastatingly brutal, or fiendishly jealous is why our creative works are so powerful and special.

We know that creating different forms and levels of detail from a single source is possible. The question is "will it be any good?", and for that we can only say we have confidence. Our systems will try and try until we get it right, because it costs very little to push in this area. The hard work is in adjusting the models to think more like a grizzled veteran than a perfectly performing AI. Once we get close on this we'll need to do a Turing Test of sorts to see if people can detect any stilted prose or badly cropped images that tip them off a machine made it instead of a person. You can imagine losing readership over things like this. It's no joke to get this wrong.

The first day that an authoring system can create a piece of Smart Information that is indistinguishable from what a person would create given the same non-trivial task is truly the first day of the Age of Smart Information.

Remixes and Mashups

One of the most important capabilities of Smart Information is the power to extract and recombine bits of objects as needed (i.e. *remixing*). Just as in hip hop music, there are no rules when it comes to how big or small these extracted and remixed parts are. The art is getting just enough and not overplaying it. Another related capability is being able to mix and match sub-elements (i.e.

mashups). Remixing relies heavily on the re-configuration of any type of source material, while mashups take elements from several different objects and combine them in unique new ways.

We could be dealing with a single datapoint or vast data universe, the requirement is the same – this functionality needs to be built into every piece of information, and our tools should make it easy to do on demand. Smart Information was envisioned as the ultimate remix and mashup format.

Setting aside copyright and fair use issues for a moment, imagine being able to combine the video from one artifact with the words and images from another as easily as you can move Legos around and snap together new formations. It's true that we can sometimes manipulate certain types of content that easily today through Copy/Paste, but more often than not, it's way more cumbersome than that. It requires a style of digital acrobatics that's too difficult for most people to bother attempting. This challenge is directly addressed by the design and architecture of Smart Information. It enables us to move into a time when just about any sub-component of a piece of information should be easy to extract through common input methods and interfaces (voice, touch, gestures, programmatically) and remixed with any other object. Imagine what the AIs will come up with here.

Living Systems

Think about how our most valuable ecosystems are formed – there's a reliance on constant change and evolution to keep the living system vibrant and its inhabitants alive. That is exactly how Smart Information's worldwide ecosystem is envisioned – as a living, breathing, growing, interconnected universe of information that is constantly evaluating itself to be up-to-date and relevant. This system leverages the Web and its functionality but is a bit different in that Smart Information objects are self-organizing, autonomous, and auto-generated parts of a large living system. The Web (for the most part) is not comprised of self-reliant code elements, but rather on pieces that need constant human attention to stay fresh.

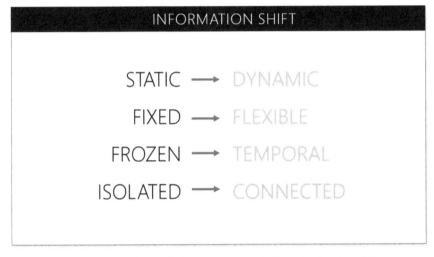

Information's shift to a living system redefines its basic attributes

The living system of information we are talking about already exists today, although only in our minds. We are able to take any piece of information or data, do the analysis on the fly, make the connections, recognize inferences, and come to conclusions as to potential next steps or state changes. Someday soon, our Smart Information will be able to do all of that without requiring people to monitor or maintain oversight. Those days only arrive with trust in place and ethics clearly understood and abided by.

Being able to rely on any piece of content being current and ready to play its part within a much large living system is about as magical as it gets.

Platforms
+ Tools

The unsung heroes of any revolution

There's no point in talking about a foundational change like this without digging into the infrastructure and tooling that will make it real. In this case, all of that is well underway, but there are some missing pieces that we need to build together.

When introducing any change to the way people commonly do things, you are immediately met with resistance – people just don't like to change. Which is exactly why we need to leverage existing patterns and behaviors to *augment rather than disrupt* what people normally do. No one wants to change the way they work, not even if it saves them time or money – it's too disruptive. There needs to be a truly compelling reason to invest the effort. In our case, there is – but it's not so immediately necessary that people would switch without question.

Smart Information is incredibly powerful and valuable, but it could easily be viewed as just an extra bonus on top of what's already there. Getting 10x more whatever during a familiar activity is our strategy for adoption – so our platforms and toolsets need to inject that perceived level of magic at the right times.

For example, being online is so intertwined with our daily lives and routines we can't imagine being without it for any reason (until the power goes out, and then we realize just how reliant we've become). Given that, any change to how we go about our day needs to come with truly noticeable improvements to those connected experiences. Checking your social media feed? Maybe you can listen to it in your AirPods instead of looking at your phone during the commute. Does that mean the author dictated the tweet? No, of course not. The AI-powered platforms and tools do that for us automatically in the background. We never notice, until we realize it didn't used to be like that. Cool.

Want to see the map of a new city much bigger than on the tiny screen of your phone? Great, see it projected at room scale with your Spatial Computing device to get a better sense for how far things are from your location. Did the original map provider have to re-create the 3D representation of the 2D map on your phone to enable this? Kinda. That was a trick question. There are some things we can't auto-generate quite as well as others, but maps are getting there quickly.

Let's dig into how we'll slipstream this new functionality into our existing work patterns. First, a few simple definitions to help clarify why each part of this equation is important.

Platforms are the underlying tech, systems, and processes that are the base layer of functionality that enable digital services and devices to do what they do. Much of our time is spent using apps or web browsers which are built on top of large platforms for networking, sharing, operating systems, communication, etc. Think of electricity as the platform that powers most of your gadgets. They wouldn't work at all without it.

Tools in this context are exactly what you'd think – the apps, programs, and services that let us create, consume, edit, manage, and get tasks done. Your mapping app is a tool. The app you use to write email is a tool. Technically, those are both services, but for all intents and purposes they are the tools that we use to get things done every day.

Platforms

In order for Smart Information to work, we need to introduce new functionality into our existing workflows and patterns. That's best done at the platform level so it comes "for free" in most cases to the person using the new functionality. That's not to say there's no cost, either financially or requirements-wise, but we like to attack these big problems at the platform level to put the onus on the developer and service provider rather than the customer.

The most obvious platform capability that's needed is some new **AI-powered functionality for helping determine current context** of Information Objects. Portions of this type of service exist today (like the *Microsoft Cognitive Services* which interprets the world around you), but not all of the capabilities we need are available in a unified way currently. A new set of platform services specifically for Smart Information support will be focused on providing on-demand AI that determines the current context someone is operating in.

Another platform level service that's needed for our base functionality is a way to keep track of Information Objects that are **geolocated in particular places** around the world or that want to react based on their current location. Having a standardized way to place or retrieve Information Objects from their position in space, anywhere in the world, is the basis of an emerging construct called the "AR Cloud". This new platform is intended to help Augmented Reality content be anchored and persistent in specific locations, according to GPS coordinates or similar means of pinpointing. When we can share and leave things for others at landmarks, or make sure that certain content is associated with physical locations, we have supercharged the ability for the world's objects and information to start telling its own story in a very contextual, spatial way.

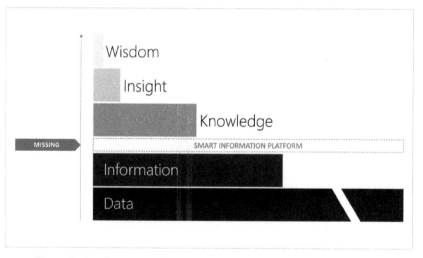

The missing layer is just above Information and below Knowledge

Faster network speeds for telecommunications, such as the emerging Fifth Generation (5G) standard, is a critical piece of infrastructure to make these Smart Information concepts come to life. High bandwidth gives us the ability to gather pieces of content together quickly on the fly. Without fast access speeds, we'd have to resort to storing everything needed by Information Objects locally (which is very suboptimal in some cases, due to footprint). For example, if we wanted to piece together levels of detail properly, some of the elements may need to be fetched in real-time to make them current (and not feel like an outdated waste of time).

Finally, we need platform capabilities to enable the ability for apps and services to **create and consume Information Objects**. That means publishing, adopting, and implementing an open, agreed upon specification for how you describe these objects. It would detail any markup, coding practices, and how we create and manipulate them programmatically. Nothing out of the ordinary here, we do this all the time for new technologies coming into being. The difference is that Information Objects require a lot of knowledge about the current environment and context. That means when these things are not available (perhaps you don't have a camera attached to your device) there must be a good fallback and degraded experience built into the platform.

Tools

Creating and working with literally dozens of information types has dominated our professional and personal lives in the modern age. We are constantly popping into and out of apps on our phones to both consume and author new pieces of information, all day, every day. The same is true for our work on laptops, headsets, and game consoles. We are exposed to all manner of digital tools wherever we happen to be in the world. And very soon, they will be able to help create and consume Smart Information.

Authoring

The key to this transformation will be updating our existing creation tools to embrace the expanded capabilities that Smart Information adds to existing digital artifacts. **Automatically adding levels of detail** to most pieces of information should be one of the first things that happens. It's a relatively straightforward process for a person to do it today (albeit tedious and highly manual), so having the AI do this in the background is a big productivity gain.

Similar services for enhancing existing content are already in place, like language translation and image transformation. These can be leveraged by Smart Information platforms to give people better choices when it comes to consuming information at the level they are most comfortable with. It's also possible that AI's Deep Learning and Reinforcement Learning algorithms will also help generate insightful new takes on the different levels of detail that a person would think of.

Auto-generating multiple forms from one original is possible

Being able to **automatically generate multiple forms** of the same digital artifact is perhaps the biggest benefit of updating the creation tools process for Smart Information. Today, we have to separately create every single version of a particular piece of information. For example, if I'm writing a research paper, I'll probably do that in Microsoft Word and then save it to Adobe Acrobat in PDF format to distribute. I may need to do some things for an academic conference submission next. That requires distilling it into an Abstract and identifying a set of keywords for searching. Next, if I want to alert my colleagues its available, I'll have to broadcast with Twitter and make a LinkedIn post. And finally, maybe I feel a Medium post is needed to get the basic ideas out there for a wider audience. Every one of those steps is a manual process today. Tomorrow, AI will be able to automatically generate many of them, if not all.

Consumption

On the flip side, in order to get widespread adoption of Smart Information in our everyday lives, we'll need to slip it into the mix of our most familiar scenarios and behavior. We can't ask people to change their behavior for no reason (they wouldn't anyway), but we can entice them to try new things if its frictionless and part of what they already do. For example, if you are reading this book and got tired of me going on and on about something, you could just ask the book for a quick summary of this chapter (if you know that capability existed – different UX problem). Similarly, being able to see all of the people, places, and things referenced within the book could be shown to you in a room-scale spatial experience, rather than in a traditionally limited use Index.

All said, we are only at the very beginning of what's possible when you inject AI, Spatial, and 5G into the information authoring and consumption models. The possibilities are limitless.

PART 4

THE
FUTURE

THE AGE OF SMART INFORMATION

Smart
Data

It's not Skynet, but our Data will become self-aware

We have all witnessed the speed at which data analytics has taken over the conversation in business, sports, and even our health. The only problem is that data can't be trusted – or more correctly put, the people flying the tools that analyze and present the data all have opinions that tend to creep into objective reports. Data has always been passive, disconnected, cold, and too easy manipulated by mistake or intention. No more.

Instead of continuing to treat our most precious modern-day commodity as though it was dumb as a rock, it is finally time to inject some intelligence into the data itself. By adding AI at the source, we not only protect the integrity of the data from misuse, but we also enable the ability for us to *see it in new ways* we hadn't considered before. All it takes is inserting Machine Learning into the mix along with some clever presentation tech to give it a sense of life. Spatial Computing engines were designed to allow for the fast construction and recombination of elements, a set of attributes from its game engine lineage. It's suits this task perfectly.

The day is coming when our artifacts are self-aware enough to fret

Self-Awareness

Let's consider how data can be enhanced with AI to provide some degree of proactive behavior to increase its usefulness. Perhaps data is like a small child who begins to learn it can start to do things for itself, without someone else's help. One step at a time, it starts to explore and see what's possible within its limits. There are missteps and tears, but over time the child learns what's possible. And in the process, they become self-aware – realizing a bit more about their capabilities, strengths, and weaknesses.

Rather than data being used as the basis for analysis, charting, and research, we need to invert the model to make data the self-aware driver instead of the passive passenger (where appropriate). Reversing data's role in the equation to be more **self-aware** and **curious** starts to treat it the same as any other piece of Smart Information. Potential performance and overhead issues aside, there's no reason why data sets shouldn't proactively be doing their own analysis or verification. Imagine each individual data point being able to protect its own integrity from attack or unauthorized use (rather than the insecure systems we build as fortresses around it today). Let's pause there for a moment and let that sink in.

Data is no longer static. It's alive.

"Smart Data" could monitor its own creation process, access requests, transit, replication, and manipulation – something we could only do at a much higher level of construct before now. The compelling reason to do this is **trust**. Above all, we need to believe that the data we are relying on to make critical decisions, conduct business, and govern gazillions of monetary transactions needs to be trustworthy and verifiable. In a world where data transactions are happening faster and faster with no human oversight, and in an incomprehensible quantity every second of every day, putting security and integrity closer to the data source is imperative.

The Blockchain gold rush is on, but is it the right security for data?

As crazy as all this may sound, we are already doing it for other high risk, high reward data scenarios. The fast growing *Blockchain* technologies used for securing financial and authoritative transactions are doing something very similar by protecting the integrity of its individual "blocks" via a distributed system of checks and balances across a network. Devised so that no one instance can be compromised without detection, Blockchain is taking the crypto market by storm, and continues to grow. By essentially putting a wrapper around each block of data, watching out for it, processing requests and attending to its needs, the system functions as an interesting model to consider. Given that example, think about how any piece of data, data set, or data center could also be encapsulated in a similar way and employ its own self-aware but coordinated efforts to stay secure and verified.

I'm not saying Blockchain tech should be used for all Smart Information implementations (necessarily), but we should learn from this area of investment and focused effort. Encapsulation of code objects is not new at all in programming circles, but inverting the model to have the object being encased driving the bus is a whole new world for data.

Conditional Access

Using curious and capable data as a backdrop, let's look at how a new kind of behavior and exploration could play out for secure information repositories.

We are constantly being challenged to identify ourselves to access every secure website or service in our lives. We are asked for credentials over and over, sometimes being spared by saved passwords, but more often than not being asked to use two factor authentication (i.e. our phones) to verify our identity. Is that bad? No, of course not. That's all needed and appreciated from a security standard, but honestly a pretty crappy experience from the human standpoint. As distasteful as that reality may be, it's not the biggest problem.

The real issue is that we have been protecting things at the wrong level. It's all or nothing. That usually means the whole site, which severely limits the kind of interactions and experiences that can be designed for that situation. Same exact situation for data. Almost all data is protected at the "collection" level, meaning a data set, database, feed, graphic, document, or service. All or nothing. No credentials, no data. Again, nothing wrong with that for some applications, but it is also something we can invert by injecting some self-awareness into the data itself. By being able to handle access requests and decide for itself what and how much it will share with whom for the current context, data is self-aware.

The ability to access data in this more granular way leads us to consider a big shift in how we think about doing collaboration and discovery. If data really was empowered and given the opportunity to explore and discover what's possible for itself, would we treat it just like that curious child we can't seem to bring ourselves to let go of? Isn't it time to stop holding everything hostage within secured sites or documents when only a few things actually need to be restricted. Think about it.

Once we push the responsibility of securing oneself all the way down into Information Objects themselves, they can exist side-by-side with other data objects that are completely unprotected or conditionally secured. That's essentially how our post-modern information ecosystems need to be built up – data sets wrapped by curious pieces of Smart Information.

Shape Dynamics

Data is worthless without context and comparison. It also needs to be put into a familiar shape that makes it easier to understand. That can be the numeric form for datapoints, charts and graphs for sales data, or familiar onscreen graphics for sports fans. Our minds arrange data according to our mental models of what it represents or the shape most familiar to us when dealing with it in the past. The shape that data takes is critical to its value. In the wrong form, it might as well be a foreign language we don't understand. But, in the right shape its value is immediate.

Smart Data objects have the ability to choose for themselves what shape to take given the current context. In many ways, that is exactly what we as Designers and Data Scientists do with data. It gets poured into shape containers like bars, pies, scatter plots, and the ever popular circular chart of doom (a great example of beauty before clarity). The shape our data is presented in says a ton about how its preparer wants us to consume it – using a particular kind of visualization brings meaning with it. We have associated the shape with the message. And that is precisely where Smart Data excels. It knows how to tell its own story (like any other piece of Smart Information) and can utilize any shape and form to achieve clarity for the viewer. That's new. Today's data is static and lifeless. What we're saying now is that data can re-flow itself into any shape that will help it convey its meaning or message for the current situation and audience.

Yes, what you just heard was the sound of a million Data Scientists scoffing. But, rest assured, the introduction of Artificial Intelligence to assist with presenting the data in the right way will change everything about Data Science and Data Visualization. What was considered an elite skill, and by some a black art, Data Visualization will be aided by AI to help choose the right shape for information based on its Machine Learning insights from doing this over and over, multiplied by the network effect. So much effort is spent today to pick the "right" shape of data only for it to be so wrong for the given audience. This is one of those cases where learning AI systems can eliminate difficult work.

Living Systems

Data, like life, can be thought of as a colossal, living, breathing system of interconnected experiences. We too often tend to look at data points or data sets in isolation, as if they came from nowhere, unconnected, silent, and alone. Nothing could be further from the truth. Every single piece of data that has ever been generated or consumed in the history of everything has come from a living system. It could be the company's monthly sales cycle, the planet's global warming, or your own medical tests. Regardless, every data point is connected and part of a very large set of other points that are not standing still in any way. Everything moves and changes. Data is a snapshot of that movement at a particular time. And so it stands to reason that we are wrongheaded to keep looking at data statically, with no hint of the motion inherent in the system it came from. True, a single data point is a perfect snapshot in time – but that's the point. It came from a continuum that is in motion.

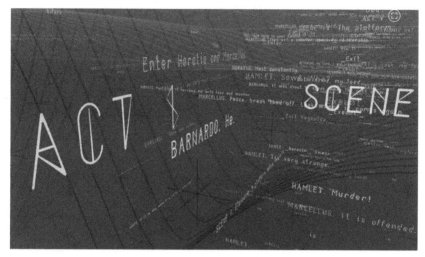

Information space are vast interactive pools of active text elements

We tend to not see the larger systems at work around us in the world. They are invisible, sometimes operating at mind-boggling speeds, and exist in a different plane – the invisible. With Smart Information, we can finally visualize and interact with these vast invisible data systems. Just as with Object-Oriented code classes, Smart Data objects understand the connection to their "parent" object and to the larger data set, stream, or original source. That gives us the hook to walk back up the connection path and explore these larger systems.

The true breakthrough here is not the stunningly beautiful renderings of these data systems, but rather the insights derived from using Machine Learning to spot the patterns in these living systems. The animations and motion of the visualizations reveal plenty about the nature, behavior, and performance of the systems, but they are nothing compared to the deep analysis possible with AI.

Smart Data Examples

Here are a few example scenarios using Smart Data to accomplish more than we can today.

Data Blade

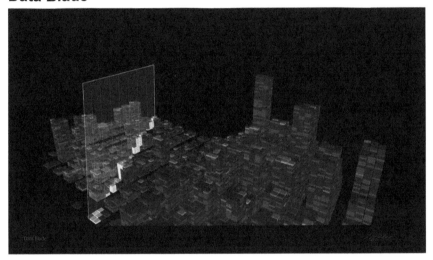

When exploring or analyzing data sets, the fastest way to scrub through the various variables and dimensions is by using a "data blade". These are shown as visual planes in 3D, but are really just a UI mechanism for moving through the values of a dimension or variable quickly. The changes in value readout in real-time as the blade is passed through the data set . These data blades are built-in parts of any Smart Data object to invite quick explorations of the values and what-if scenarios

Datacenter

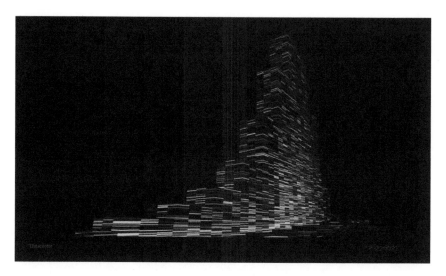

Data will become self-aware and self-organizing, which means it will gravitate toward other similar types of data or situations where there are like-minded data sets. These mirror-world repositories are called datacenters, much like their physical building equivalents. These digital datacenters do the same type of management and maintenance of their data tenants as the real-world equivalent.

Multi-Dimensional Data

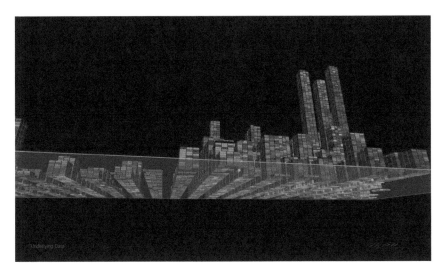

Combining the data blade and datacenter, this example is illustrating how you can isolate particular datasets and examine them from any angle. In this particular example, the data is from the 2010 US Census, filtered to show aspects of income and education level. The interaction of note is the ability to see underneath the surface level data to where you suspect something not quite right. Exploration is quick, but analysis is tedious as other methods.

Geoshaping Data

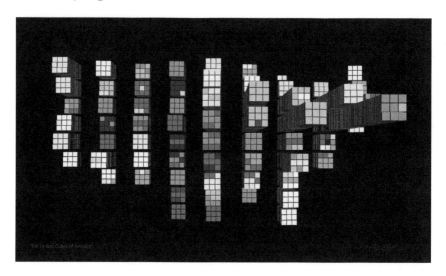

Maps and geospatial relationships are one of the easiest ways for people to recognize and consume data. Putting datasets into maps and map-like constructs is a great way to create the sense of familiarity that people desire. This particular example plots income and education onto a map of the USA. Higher piles indicate more of the desired variable.

Being able to self-organize into these familiar geo shapes helps the Smart Data be recognized and explored.

Data Towers

There's a similarity between walking through New York City while seeing the massive towering skyscrapers and engaging in a virtual tour of your data sets within Virtual Reality or Mixed Reality. The key experience aspect with this is the scale and sense of perspective that these so-called Data Towers bring. It's hard to undersell the positive impression and sense of familiarity when exploring data in this form.

Not for every application, Data Towers can be useful when a sense of huge scale is useful in engaging people who are exploring. This data shape is one of the best for initial exploration

.

Data Outliers

There are frequently "outliers" in datasets – values or datapoints that seem to be out of bounds or unexpected for some reason. These are typically hidden within large datasets, sometimes never coming to light. They are hard to spot. With Smart Data shaping, we can elevate these outliers to be easy to spot visually or in analysis.

In this particular example, the outlier occupies the penthouse of a data tower, showing off its specialness with a brightly lit space.

Learning Data

One of the key differentiators with Smart Data its ability to learn in the background, instead of just sitting doing nothing. Individual datapoints or entire datasets can use their AIs to run jobs where new insights are explored or related items tagged and associated.

In this example, the datapoints that are actively learning are shown brightly colored.

Data Fog

As Charlie Fink likes to say, "the world will be painted with data" – or in this example, the world will be permeated by a Data Fog. Drifting into and out of most everything, Smart Data can take a physical form like this to illustrate mood or surface emotion. The effect itself can either be made of data or just a visual special effect to augment the presentation of other data.

In the above scene, the buildings in the background are actually Datascrapers themselves. The Data Fog is an additional layer of values that work with the base dataset.

Data Storm

When too much data is accessed by or injected into a database at one time, it's a scenario referred to as a Data Storm. The incoming data may or may not be captured properly by the accessor. Visual cues are present when this condition exists, such as a violent weather look and storm characteristics such as blowing wind, rain, or dark threatening skies while the situation continues.

Data Bridge

Connecting different types of data sets and making them presentable is one of the talents of Smart Data. This is done by building bridges between the databases or datasets and exchanging elements as needed. The bridges are dynamic, so you can see them being deployed across voids or bodies of water.

In the example, the city in the distance at the end of the Data Bridge is actually comprised of hundreds of Datascrapers.

Smarter People

Does this information make me look smart?

Is using a calculator on a math test cheating? Of course not, unless you were specifically told not to use it before the test started. That said, doesn't it feel just a bit like cheating when you don't have to calculate all that stuff in your head or longhand? Didn't think so. We've all become so used to using our modern tools for whatever tasks they happen to be good at, who cares? Why should I have to tax my tired brain any more than I have to. We have calculating machines for that. And so it goes…

We usually get over whatever objection people first raise to augmenting our innate intelligence with some mechanical, digital, or metaphysical power up. What first looks like an unnecessary cheat or extravagant indulgence for laziness soon starts seeming like a good idea. And why not. It's getting you something you do another way, but much easier – so what's not to like? The same will be true of Smart Information.

Augmented Intelligence

At some point, you'll probably need to know what this book was really about if someone asks you at work. Yes, you could have read this entire book or done your own "research" on Wikipedia – but why not just ask the book itself to explain what it was about? "Tell me more about you" would be all it takes. And by the way, yes I know that Alexa or Siri might be able to help me. Might. Probably not. But someday. The point is that instead of using a super broad web search lookup of a search term, we can just go straight to the source and get our question answered – just the way you or I would do it in the real world. We'd ask a person who seemed like they might know, and then answer authoritatively ourselves when asked as if we had actually read it. Why not. You look good, the other person got their answer. Everybody is happy. And best of all, no one seemed to care that Smart Information was the thing that helped you look smarter.

The real advantage to asking information or digital artifacts our questions directly is to gain additional insights through their singular focus. Web searches are great at instantly returning thousands of results in a ~~paid-for-first~~ relevance kinda way, not necessarily what you're looking for. It takes a fair bit of practice to master the art of search term construction to get exactly what you're after.

Treating our digital artifacts as *intelligence augmentation tools* rather than just words and pictures is a giant mindshift, but an easy thing to start doing. Thinking about it too much overcomplicates everything. Just do it. Next time you need to know how many widgets were sold in Q4 in the UK, just quietly ask the company logo on that presentation you're looking at on your smartphone.

That logo is a summary level of detail that's connected to the rest of the company's digital infrastructure these days (because we can represent the entire company as a single digital object thanks to Smart Information), and as such can be queried to retrieve any other piece of information – like the Q4 sales report for the UK. As it reports back through the AirPod in your left ear that 13,806 units were sold, you pipe up and impress the manager with your command of the numbers. Mission accomplished. Feeling pretty good about that promotion now…

Whoah. That promo is in the bag. Thanks Information Objects!

And so it goes with Smart Information – the more pervasive it is in our lives, the more it recedes into the background as just another tool to get what we need done, done. It's not merely a way to look smart by using instant recall to pull quotes out of thin air on demand (although it does do that), Smart Information makes us all smarter through its ability to adjust itself to our needs, not make us figure it out every time we encounter each other.

Visualizing Decisions

Making good decisions isn't science. There's a fair degree of life experience, instinct, mojo, and ability to project possible outcomes mixed into any decision that turned out well or not. Having some data to help you make that decision is always a good thing, but that same data should never be used to make the call for you. That's where your ability to visualize outcomes is handy. Some of the smartest people you'll come across in life are blessed with not only intelligence, but *vision*. They can see how things will play out in their mind's eye in an instant (some call that parenting). The important part is that we can conjure up the imagery as needed to "see" an outcome in own thoughts or hear it coming out of our mouths as we explain to someone else.

You really liked that last time you had it. Try it again?

Information Objects have the ability to compute and simulate outcomes of specified scenarios, much like a configurator on a website is programmed to show you what-if calculations for loans at several different rates, terms, and down payments. It's a way to see the outcome of decisions using specific variable values. By visualizing different aspects of decisions and scenarios from different angles, altitudes, and perspectives we can make more informed and enlightened decisions based on those projected outcomes. Many of us do this already in our own ways.

By using Smart Information as a medium for exploration, the decision outcomes themselves are finally visible and sharable with other people for input. You could hear the scenario played out for you audibly in your earbud, see it projected onto a wall as a video, or immerse yourself in the simulation via Spatial Computing and Multi-Dimensional techniques. The possibilities here are vast, as you can have scenarios play out audio-only or visually in 2D, 3D, VR, or any combination with stunning effect.

Potential outcomes are no longer trapped within people's own mental models. Possible outcomes fueled by simulation are now visible to anyone once released and published. We will be able to make better decisions once the original information artifacts that prompted the questions can be used as tools themselves.

Nothing wrong with being the smartest person in the room.

Example Scenarios

The are several common situations where we have nothing like Smart Information today. Here's how those could play out.

Active Schedule

When attending industry conferences, there's always a rush to figure out how to get to the next interesting speaker (if you can find one in the program) and spot what they'll actually be talking about.

The better way to think about this using Smart Information, is to bring the speaker to you first. See what they're talking about, where the room is in relation to your seat in the hotel lobby, and how long until the session starts. It's configured the way you would expect, with direct links to the speaker's bio, presentation deck, and reviews of prior sessions.

Good example of making the information work for us instead of the other way around.

Meeting Presence

You knew this one would show up, and for good reason – we have all been in that meeting where people were late joining the call remotely, someone was not sure where the file to present was, and you just can't feel good about talking without seeing them.

In this scenario, instead of just using PowerPoint or Excel for their presentations, the remote team opted for high quality holograms to communicate as clearly as possible what the quality control issues are. The photorealistic look of the robot and dog are far better than seeing something over a regular video messaging call, and they are interactive so that subparts can be selected and queried upon. Everything is hooked up to the manufacturing database, so rather than just a dashboard that reads out metrics, the team can dig in on this one.

Immersive Datacenter

There's no more powerful way to deliver data-based information than a fully immersive data experience. People have a natural fascination with holograms and data in 3D. When familiar data is presented at room scale, with perspective, something magical happens. You are transfixed and ready to explore more deeply than any 2D chart you've ever seen.

In this example, people are completely inside their Datacenter server data stack, are able to take action on error conditions, and investigate other related areas quickly due to proximity. The data set itself is secured and managed as we discussed earlier, with Blockchain or similar base technologies and AI that allows the data to be more self-aware and query its own health.

Book Holograms

We have all seen movies where some 3D characters jump off the pages of the magazine or book and proceed to tear your house apart. That's now very possible and available for not much money. This was in many ways the most straightforward application of Smart Information technology, and in others, the most difficult.

Starting from the place of wanting to see my book act itself out, we can see the Mixed Reality holograms involved in a scene. That technology allows for placement onto flat surfaces, but should remain persistant. You can walk around and observe the holograms from various perspectives. They definitely add to the book reading experience, and in deft hands, can be a great storytelling device.

Lunch Activities

In this scene during lunch time, there are three very different scenarios unfolding, each with its own special aspect to it.

The ladies on the far left are discussing the debut of a new wearable dress at Fashion Week. One of them noticed a mention of it in her social media feed and choose to project it onto the tabletop where her friend was sitting with her. They can twirl the dress around to inspect the electronics and effects, or read the news article.

The gentleman in the foreground is enjoying catching up on a soccer match he missed the prior evening. His preference is to watch it on a tabletop rather than his smartphone or tablet, because it can be spread out and the player's movements easier to see. He can sit back and enjoy his sandwich while rotating the field of play.

And finally, two friends in the background are arguing over who has the best lunch special in the nearby area.

Smarter People

In the end, we are all only as smart as we want to be. No amount of technology or magic is going to change the way we think about the world or each other. There are things we can show you to make you think twice about using that plastic container or eating that burger, but you control what you do and believe.

The real breakthrough may come when we realize its time to put the tech down and start to talk to one another again, face to face, with only our words, expressions, and emotions to guide us forward. That's when we truly learn and grow into Smarter People.

Smartest World

"If you live in this world, you're feelin' the change of the guard." – Becker and Fagen

Information is not just a layer that lies on top of the physical world around us – it's part of our world's fabric, as inseparable from our existence as air. Hard to see it that way sometimes if you consider the mediums used to communicate it and the vessels used to hold it. But it's true – people need good information to push on in pursuit of our own hopes and dreams, and bad information to make those mistakes that help us learn. It's at once the lifeblood of the 21st century and the bane of our existence. There's no separating us from our reliance upon it, just as people can barely fathom being offline for a few hours. Trying to evolve that information we rely so heavily on toward a more intelligent and aware companion makes a lot of sense in this world.

Smart Information is our new "digital air".

Let's take a quick look at how this fundamental transformation in the way we perceive and interact with information, and the world around us, plays out in the physical spaces we exist in.

Active Spaces

"Don't let the door hit you on the way out" was a nice way to say get out of my office right this second. Turns out, that may not be just a cute expression for much longer. Doors will automatically open and close without you asking. The physical spaces we live and work in are being transformed right along with our digital tools. Sensors, microphones, cameras, haptics, networks, and reconfigurable furnishings are being infused into new construction and retrofits every day. Our spaces have also moved from being passive containers to active stages.

Spaces will help us with the little things

Entering a room will not be a surprise to the room. It will have heard you were coming from all the other sensors in the area, and use its AI to adjust itself to your preferred setup for lighting, acoustics, connectivity, displays, etc. In a similar fashion, your information will also be aware of the room or space you are currently in and react accordingly. That's where the contextual intelligence we've talked about comes in.

If you are in space with bad lighting, your information will know it from its connection to the sensors in the room and be presented in a form that doesn't need good light. If you're in an extremely noisy public place when trying to connect with someone, your information will be visually presented to sidestep the noise issue. Nothing mysterious about this. It's straightforward when you have all of this tech at your disposal. The difference is that the space is now an actor and participant in your day, every day, from now on.

Our information will be able to control aspects about the room to make itself "heard" in the best way when asked. That's a complete reversal of today's PowerPoint presentation culture, where the room is as dumb as it gets and the slides not much better. Smart Information now turns any room into an active space to be utilized in communicating clearly.

Reactive Places

Walking into a place that plays off your emotion, tone, and agenda will take interactions to another level. That's also a pretty good definition for a Reactive Place, which serves mainly as an active participant in goings on rather than an inanimate structure. A Reactive Place is in some ways the polar opposite of an Active Space. One is demonstrably involved in what's happening within its bounds (Reactive Place), and the other acts silently to help enhance the overall experience (Active Space).

Large outdoor spaces are already reacting to people

Another simple differentiator is Reactive Places are designed to be engaging immersive experiences infused with Smart Information as actors, much like a modern exhibit space in a children's museum has props and stations. These spaces use all the same tech and techniques as Active Spaces to provide data about the current state of the room itself as input to Smart Information objects (to help them make decisions about how to communicate effectively for the given situation). But, Reactive Places feel like a very different animal – a vibrant and curious third party, deeply involved in the conversations you're having.

Another interesting aspect of these Reactive Spaces is the infusion of Smart Information as sculptures or exhibits. Given our ability to use Spatial tech for deeply immersive experiences, this kind of setup is the optimal for next generation level installations. Multi-dimensional by nature, these types of spaces are attuned to the unique attributes of the individuals within them, not satisfied to present itself the same for everyone. The equivalent of what used to be envisioned and built by teams within our greatest adventure parks is now available for information explorers rather than roller coaster junkies. Who knew Smart Information could be the basis of a thrilling adventure space? Just wait until you have your very own.

Dying Planet

In the end, it may turn out that the most impactful use of Smart Information will be to give voice to the planet itself. It certainly appears she's angry and has a lot to say. That should be clear from all the horrendous natural disasters and loss of life we have experienced over the last decade. The world is changing in ways we could have never imagined as young children, and it is finally time to try and do something about it.

There's so much more to say than we normally do

There may be no better container for conveying the complex stories about our planet changing than the flexible and multi-dimensional Smart Information. It's ability to truly reach people by conveying key points at the right altitude and level of detail for the audience is why we need to invest in learning how to get the most out this medium.

With the ability to convert any text into the supported languages, we finally have a universal translator for getting our messages out to anyone and everyone who is interested in our observations, assertions, and genuine passion for the world we all share. This is the time to put our technological advancements to best use by sharing our messages of hope. We cannot sit idly by while the planet slowly melts away before our eyes.

Smart Information has an important role to play in the future of the planet, and so do you.

All of us are so different in how we respond to things, always in our own ways. Important messages need to reach you in the ways that can capture your attention and move your soul. We have tons of work to do in this area, so the more we can do behind-the-scenes to make information accessible to everyone around the world the better chance of success we have in reaching them.

Through the combination of Artificial Intelligence, Spatial Computing, and Human Ingenuity, we have the perfect storm of elements to create the most compelling immersive storytelling tool for the informational aspects of our biggest global challenges. Let's all do our part to learn how to best utilize these new approaches and technologies to tell these stories of hope and change before it's too late. And make no mistake, the hour is getting late.

Smart Information ignites an information revolution that will help save the world, but we need your passion to make it happen. I'm in for trying to use Smart Information to power those messages.

There's a revolution calling.
Are you in?

CLOSING THOUGHTS

Deceptively powerful and stunningly beautiful, this monumental leap forward in conveying information effectively has always been right there in front of us, waiting to be unlocked, hiding in plain sight. All it took was the convergence of human ingenuity, Artificial Intelligence, and the rise of a medium capable of magic.

Welcome to the age of "Smart Information".

Until next time

UPDATES

You have my sincere thanks for reading this book. Please follow me on **Twitter** for bonus content and new posts. Would also really appreciate you sharing your thoughts about this book with friends.

Or feel free to reach out to me any of these ways:

BOOK SITE
TheAgeOfSmartInformation.com

INSTAGRAM
instagram.com/mpell_futuristicdesign/

LINKEDIN
linkedin.com/in/mikepell

MY SITE
futuristic.com

ACKNOWLEDGEMENTS

Thank you.

Yes, I do mean *you*.

Do you ever go to the Acknowledgments page of a new book to see if the author remembered to thank you for inspiring the most important part? Yeah, me too. Sorry, but you won't find your name here either :/

The truth is, there are way too many special people for me to thank properly for their inspiration, dedication, and friendship. You all know exactly who you are, and how much **I truly appreciate you** (because I tell you all the time). But still, thank you again.

It's a real privilege to be able to share some things that I've learned with an interested audience – whether that's just one person (like you) or a room full. A sincere thank you for staying with me.

If you keep reading, I'll keep writing.
Please share what you think online…

ABOUT THE AUTHOR

 **M. Pell**

Bold, insightful, and uncompromising, M. Pell is recognized as a world-class designer and industry thought leader. Pell's first book "Envisioning Holograms" is considered a must-have for tomorrow's most influential storytellers and explorers. This forward-looking book "The Age of Smart Information" details how the fundamental nature of information is changing due to AI and Spatial Computing.

A lifelong Designer/Coder, Pell has consistently been out on the leading edge of design and innovation in the high-tech industry. Career highlights include helping invent Adobe Acrobat and PDF, pioneering 3D type tools for Pixar RenderMan, and leading the Design effort worldwide for The Microsoft Garage.

Learn more about M. Pell at futuristic.com

| 1989 | 1993 | 1995 | 2001 | 2014 | 2017 |

INDEX

Oh, sorry. Did you think there would be an Index?

Next time :-)

If you are now interested in reading M. Pell's first book called *"Envisioning Holograms"* about the design of Mixed Reality experiences, you can find many places to purchase it at the site below and some great reviews from people who work in the space.

BOOK SITE

www.EnvisioningHolograms.com

NOTES

SKETCHES

INSPIRATION

Lightning Source UK Ltd.
Milton Keynes UK
UKHW022233310122
397978UK00003B/206/J